Having known for nearly twenty years the man about whom this book is written, I was privy to many of the lessons he learned on the way to heaven. Mike was indeed a force of unusual character; however, this story—told by his son Michael Jr.—is a powerful encouragement to those of us who may doubt our place or feel inadequate when it comes to advancing God's kingdom. While Mike was no doubt called and gifted, this story is about *the greatness of the God who called and gifted him.* It is ultimately the story of God's redemptive work in the world, which he has chosen to accomplish through flawed and weak creatures. Mike would be contemptuous of any other perspective.

S. MICHAEL CRAVEN, president of H.I.S. BridgeBuilders

Reading *Lessons on the Way to Heaven* reintroduced me to a man who impacted my life in a profound way. Mike Fechner didn't preach a sermon; he lived it 24/7. As I read, I found myself recommitting to the unselfish principles that guided his life. These pages keep alive a legacy of surrender and authenticity. Caution: Know that this book will interfere with comfortable living and challenge you to live your life differently.

DAN DEAN, lead singer of Phillips, Craig, and Dean

Authentically challenging! This is an important book for Christians living in the opulence of Western church culture. Michael Fechner Jr. does a masterful job sharing the life of one of this generation's heroes of the faith.

DAN TRIPPIE, pastor of Restoration Church, Buffalo, New York

Lessons on the Way to Heaven is a monument to courage and humility, rooted in the love and grace of Jesus Christ. Mike Fechner's is a capacious mind and heart, and I was deeply touched and guided by the many graces of God that recur again and again in this lovely and tender book. Its eloquence and aspiration make it a joy to read.

TIM GOEGLEIN, vice president of external relations and senior advisor to the president, Focus on the Family

Mike Fechner was a personal friend whom I dearly loved and had the greatest respect for. His story is a remarkable witness to the power of the gospel to shatter our preconceived notions and tear down walls of our own making that are the result of a fallen and broken world. This is a wonderful book I couldn't put down. Pick it up and start reading—and you will see what I mean.

DANIEL L. AKIN, president of Southeastern Baptist Theological Seminary, Wake Forest, North Carolina

The Mike Fechner who comes alive in this book was an ocular demonstration of a disciple of Jesus seeking to transform persons and families throughout our global community. I witnessed the brotherhood that existed between my husband, E. K. Bailey, a black man, and Mike Fechner, a white man. Our family was recipients of his love when my husband suffered with three bouts of cancer. How honorable for a son to embrace his father's lessons, as his father emulated his heavenly Father. Mike's passion, purpose, and perseverance exude from each chapter. Read it! Discuss it! Live it! We as believers are on our way to our heavenly home!

SHEILA BAILEY, speaker, revivalist, teacher, and president of Sheila B. Ministries

In 1998, Mike Fechner led my wife and me to Christ and then discipled us for three years. He did not just talk the talk; he walked the walk of Jesus' great commandment to love God and love others. This book will challenge you to reject cultural Christianity and should be read by any Christian who is serious about walking as Jesus walked. I want my whole congregation to read it.

BILL BORINSTEIN, senior pastor of Harvest Bible Chapel North, Phoenix, Arizona

My favorite stories in history are about people like Lord Anthony Ashley Cooper and George Mueller—people who risked everything for Christ and for the sake of the poor. Michael Fechner Jr. has done us an immense favor by sharing a story for anyone who longs for the true greatness described by Jesus: "Anyone who wants to be first must be the very last, and the servant of all." Mike's commitment to Jesus, to his family, to his church, to his pastor, and to the poor astonished me. I knew him as a prophet who was as quick to laugh as he was to weep and pray. He was often radiant and always relentless. The poor of Dallas and elsewhere loved him. His family honored him. He enriched the kingdom of God. Oh, how I miss him. His life still challenges mine. His story should change you.

DR. BOB BAKKE, teaching pastor at Hillside Church, Bloomington, Minnesota

Mike Fechner lived with his feet firmly planted in the soil of human experience and struggle, yet his heart was captured with the radiant beams of heaven's glory. He loved God and served people with a bright smile and infectious laughter. This book tells his story and offers a challenge to all who dare journey here to write a story with their lives that is greater than themselves. Michael Fechner Jr. learned some painful yet life-enriching lessons from a father who took great risks to live gospel truth in daily life. This book urges us not only live for today but also to love and serve with eternity in view.

DR. DAVID H. MCKINLEY, pastor-teacher, Warren Baptist Church, Augusta, Georgia

I knew Mike Fechner well and loved him deeply. If ever there was the "real deal," it was Mike. Michael Jr. has captured the essence of who his dad was and his life message in a way that can only be described as powerful and inspired. This is not just the story of a good man facing death but ultimately the story of a gracious Lord who walked with him. You will read it and weep, but you will also read it and reap!

O. S. HAWKINS, author of *The Joshua Code*, *The Jesus Code*, and *The James Code*

Never have I been around a man who loved Jesus and people more than Mike Fechner. His life was an example of what it means to be totally surrendered to the will of God. His heart for the least and his desire to live by faith challenged and inspired all who knew him. *Lessons on the Way to Heaven* gives an inside glimpse of the grace of God in Mike's life that made him to be a kingdom bridge builder.

JARRETT STEPHENS, teaching pastor at Prestonwood
Baptist Church, Plano, Texas

Usually we read biographies about people we never had the privilege to know. With *Lessons on the Way to Heaven*, it's different. I saw these lessons lived out, talked out, prayed out—and they impacted me deeply. I read this book in one sitting because I felt as though Mike was talking to me and challenging me to be more like Jesus once again. The lessons Mike learned and shared so openly are the lessons we all need to learn.

JEFF YOUNG, minister of spiritual development,
Prestonwood Baptist Church, Plano, Texas

Michael Fechner was an amazing man who was 100 percent sold out to bringing restoration to urban Dallas. He inspired and challenged anyone he came into contact with. I'm so glad I had the opportunity to know him and even more grateful that his vision and principles have been captured in this book so others can be inspired too. Be ready to have your assumptions about urban ministry challenged and turned upside down. *Lessons on the Way to Heaven* is a much-needed road map for churches that want to see their cities transformed.

KEVIN EZELL, president of North American
Mission Board, Southern Baptist Convention

This book is more than a son sharing and honoring his father's story. Michael Fechner Jr. challenges all of us to live with purpose, to have an eternal focus, and to keep an eye on the next generation—a person's legacy. Michael picks up where his father left off—pointing people to Jesus Christ, our hope and glory.

LARRY TAYLOR, PhD, Head of School at
Prestonwood Christian Academy, Plano, Texas

LESSONS

ON THE WAY TO

HEAVEN

WHAT MY FATHER TAUGHT ME

MICHAEL FECHNER JR.

WITH BOB WELCH

ZONDERVAN

Lessons on the Way to Heaven
Copyright © 2016 by Michael Fechner Jr.

Requests for information should be addressed to:
Zondervan, 3900 Sparks Dr. SE, Grand Rapids, Michigan 49546

Library of Congress Cataloging-in-Publication Data

Names: Fechner, Michael, 1988-
Title: Lessons on the way to heaven : what my father taught me /
    Michael Fechner, Jr.; with Bob Welch.
Description: Grand Rapids: Zondervan, 2016.
Identifiers: LCCN 2015027968 | ISBN 9780310343660 (hardcover) |
    ISBN 9780310343691 (ebook) | ISBN 9780310065562 (mobile app)
Subjects: LCSH: Fechner, Michael, 1961-2014. | Christian biography—
    Texas—Dallas.
Classification: LCC BR1725,F435 F43 2016 | DDC 277.3/083092—dc23
    LC record available at http://lccn.loc.gov/2015027968

Published in association with the literary agency of WordServe Literary Group,
Ltd., www.wordserveliterary.com.

Cover design: James W. Hall IV
Cover illustration: © Hong Li/iStockphoto®
Interior imagery: © Bryan Solomon/Shutterstock
Interior design: Kait Lamphere

First Printing November 2015 / Printed in the United States of America

To my mom, Laura Fechner—
the silent hero.

*Life can only be understood backwards; but it
must be lived forwards.*
    —Danish philosopher Søren Kierkegaard

Do not be anxious about anything . . .
                —Philippians 4:6

CONTENTS

PREFACE

:::::

This is a story about a once-wealthy man who thought he had it all but realized the "all" he had was nothing. White, privileged, and proud, he underwent a huge life change after an encounter with a woman who was black, poor, and humble.

I know the story because the man was my father.

There's a danger in writing a book about your dad: As a reader, you may assume it's going to be a never-ending love song to the old man, a subjective meandering of gush and mush. So, right away, let me alleviate any fears you might have: Mike Fechner wasn't perfect.

He was always late. *Always.* Like Robert De Niro, the girlfriend's father in *Meet the Parents*, he could be insufferably controlling. He'd embarrass the heck out of the family in a restaurant, chatting up this person or that. He could speak before esteemed leaders at the White House on the National Day of Prayer but, back home, pout over a "Free Parking" ruling in a game of Monopoly.

That said, he had the courage to let God reinvent him completely. He went from a self-seeking Yuppie to an other-oriented servant. He felt no less privileged to be praying with gang members than with heads of state at the White House.

And he did some of his most amazing living after he learned he was dying.

So, the reason I'm writing about my father isn't that he was flawless. It's that he had an incredible story to tell about God's life-changing power but isn't around to tell it. And people kept saying to me, "Someone has to share his story."

Enter me. Aside from my mom, Laura, I'm the person on this planet who knew Mike Fechner Sr. best. I'm twenty-seven, the oldest of four Fechner children, the husband of Caitlin. I'm a Bible study teacher at Prestonwood Baptist Church, where my father used to serve. I graduated in 2010 from the University of Texas and am now a law student at Southern Methodist University.

Beyond my own insight gleaned from having known the man for nearly thirty years, I will rely heavily on my father's written memories, which were considerable; on written accounts from others; and on numerous interviews with those who knew him well.

He wanted to tell the story; in fact, even as he battled the rigors of cancer a book proposal of his had been accepted. But the contract from Zondervan arrived on April 14, 2014—a date that will forever be etched in my memory.

It was the day of my father's funeral.

—*Michael Fechner Jr., Dallas, Texas*
February 2015

One

ALL SHOWROOM,
NO WAREHOUSE

:::::

Plano, Texas, and my father went together like brisket and ribs. In 1989, when our story begins, not only did our family live in Plano—I was a year old—but both the city and my father were on the rise. During the 1980s alone, the population of the once-sleepy Dallas suburb doubled, as big companies such as JCPenney and Frito-Lay plunked down their corporate headquarters there.

People dressed for success, my father among them. This, after all, was North Dallas. If cops were patrolling neighborhoods, it wasn't to quell drug deals, but to issue warnings to rogue sprinkler users during droughts. Blink, and you'd miss a couple of new housing developments pop up. Long an opportunist, Dad had bagged his job as an insurance underwriter to sell something he realized every one of these new houses needed—security systems.

His father, Ruben, had started the business in San Antonio. Though Dad was only in his mid-twenties, his Dallas branch of the business went crazy. Soon he was on his way to becoming a millionaire—and becoming a workaholic in the process.

Dad and my mother, Laura, drove a BMW. For her birthday, he bought her a diamond and gold watch, later surprising her with a mink coat. Having a baby son, me, didn't slow Mom and Dad down a bit; I'd been to Europe before I was potty-trained. Mom and Dad were a great-looking couple. My dad was lanky, six foot one, and deeply tanned; Mom had strawberry red hair and shy southern charm. "We looked like we walked straight out of a magazine," my father wrote.

They attended a large evangelical church—membership was climbing toward ten thousand—whose pastor leaned toward preaching a "prosperity gospel": if you're faithful, God will bless you. If many who attended Prestonwood Baptist were sincere and committed in their faith, my father was not among them. He was attracted to the church because it was a "Who's Who of North Dallas Business"—wealthy bankers, big-time developers, oil people, and the like.

He began to climb the ranks of the lay leaders. He sang solos during Sunday worship services. Got on the deacon board; at age twenty-six, he was one of the youngest ever. He even taught a Bible class, his lack of spiritual depth masked by his abundance of charisma.

You've heard of people who can "own the room"? Dad owned every room he stepped foot in. He was part salesman, part baby-kissing politician, and part verbose pastor. All of this at a church that, given my father's go-go-go lifestyle at the time, was the perfect fit. It was among the fastest-growing churches in America.

"Prestonwood was a larger-than-life place," he said of the four-thousand-seat church, "and I deftly positioned myself in its center."

Looking back, my father had emerged as an individual microcosm of Plano—full of unabashed pride, unchecked growth, and unlimited potential. But he was so miserable he would stay up nights in anguish. Deep in his soul, he knew he was living a lie.

"It was a facade," he wrote. "I worked long hours, day and night. Friendships were all about comparing what we had with others and affirming each other's material possessions. On the outside, we were beautiful people living in a beautiful place doing beautiful things, but inside, the pit opened wide, and it was asking more and more of my soul."

At age twenty-eight—just a year older than I am now—he looked in the mirror and didn't see Mike Fechner; he saw the rich young ruler Jesus had admonished to sell all he had, give to the poor, and "follow me." Or the prodigal son, who had turned his back on God's ways. Or the one he identified with most—Jacob, who was known for his deception.

"I was a deceiver," he wrote. "All showroom. No warehouse."

For a two-week period, unable to sleep, he stayed up long after my mom had gone to bed, weeping in misery. "God," he prayed, "I don't really know you. I'm so far away. I can't overcome these lies. Help me. Please help me."

That's the first lesson my father learned: That God listens.

That God cares about us. That God answers our prayers, though not necessarily how we might envision him doing so.

My dad was about to undergo a radical life change whose catalyst was a woman who couldn't be more different from him. Not that digging out of this dark hole of deceit would be easy. After all, he had been digging that hole since roughly the day he was born.

Two

COOKING THE BOOKS

::::

At age five, my dad and his twin brother, Mel, were sifting through a garbage dumpster on the military post in Virginia where their father—my grandfather—was a colonel. They found a bag of individually wrapped candy. Uncle Mel wanted to eat it. Dad wanted to sell it.

"My brother and I are selling candy," he told the person at the first house they went to. "All proceeds will go toward planting flowers in the neighborhood."

Ka-ching. An easy fifty cents. The person behind the next doorbell went down just as easy. And on and on.

Mel didn't like the duplicity—*what flowers?*—but went along with the ploy. When Ruben, their older brother, heard of the plan, he demanded a third of the take or he'd talk. (Extortion at an early age.) My dad refused. Ruben squealed. Mel and Dad were forced to retrace their steps and apologize to all they had duped.

But here's how hardened my dad's heart was at that tender age: "There was no contriteness in my heart, no sorrow for my lies," he wrote. "Only a strengthened resolve not to get caught next time."

His thirst for getting rich was triggered by a desire to be like his granddad, a confident, successful doctor who always carried around rolls of bills. It was never about what the money could buy; all he ever wanted was a rolltop desk. A strange desire for a little boy, yes, but as you'll come to find out, Dad was anything but conventional. You see, the money was about how it would make him *look* and *feel*. Important. Cool. Successful. From the beginning, image was everything.

A year before my dad's father shipped out to Vietnam in 1968, the family was stationed in Virginia and went to a church where the pastor genuinely cared about the spiritual lives of the kids in the congregation.

One night, after hearing the pastor speak on John 3:16, my father came home with a heavy heart. "I already knew I was a manipulator," he wrote. "Lying came easy. If Jesus came back that night, I knew I wasn't saved, and that thought scared the life out of me."

He raced into the family room where his parents were watching TV. "I need to know Jesus," he said in a small voice.

They explained how that was possible. The next day, he and his brother Mel prayed to be forgiven and to welcome Christ into their lives. But not surprisingly, his faith didn't grow much deeper. In Sunday school, kids were given an array of pins as rewards for attendance, memorizing verses, and the like. My dad's shirts soon were as well decorated as a five-star general, but he was just like the young man he would grow up to be. "I was," he said, "a pretender."

As he got older, what continued to sink his integrity was greed. He and his brothers were to keep track of the money they made from doing chores and tithe 10 percent at church. "But I hated the idea of tithing," he wrote. "It was *my* money, not God's."

At ten, he was "cooking the books" like a tax cheater, under-reporting his income so he could justify paying less of a tithe. With his dad away in Vietnam and the family having moved to Texas, he was allowed to play bingo at Fort Worth's Colonial Country Club, where his granddad was a member. As his blotted numbers started to line up in his favor, his heart pounded with anticipation.

"Bingo!" he yelled. He had won a $200 jackpot, but when his mother made him split it with brothers Mel and Ruben, he fumed.

His grandparents—not churchgoers at the time—would host huge poker games, and my dad was allowed to play. When a great-uncle offered him pointers, he listened with the intensity of an attendee at a get-rich-quick seminar in a Hilton ball-room. And it paid off. He walked off with a handful of cash one evening.

This is it, he remembered thinking. *This is what I want in life—and more.*

Three

EMPATHY
FOR OTHERS

:::::

I'm only twenty-seven, but I've lived long enough to know that, like some Starbucks coffee orders, people tend to be complicated blends of flavors, temperatures, and consistencies. Not all good. Not all bad. My dad, as a kid, was the same way. If he had a greedy side that became a part of who he was as an adult, he also had a heart that did the same.

In Virginia, one of his classmates was a special-needs boy named Harold. He was big, angry, and didn't shower too often. He liked to purposely run into other kids with his wheelchair. Not surprisingly, nobody was quick to help get Harold around in that chair. Instead, they returned evil for evil. They teased him or shunned him but did nothing to try to connect with him.

Except for my dad. He was new at the school and didn't have friends to play with at recess, so he figured he might as well help Harold out. He genuinely liked the boy. It was as if he could see through Harold's anger to the kid inside. Harold wanted to swing on the swings and climb on the monkey bars like everyone else, but would never get that chance.

As a boy, Dad heard a story about his mother when she was a teenager in Texas. She had been asked to go grocery shopping with the family's black maid. When they were finished shopping, my grandmother invited the woman into a drugstore to get a Coke. The store's owner was furious.

"Get out of my store, never come back, and never bring this type of person into my place!" he said. "You are not welcome here! Ever!"

My grandmother was aghast. She didn't understand what was happening. She paid for the Cokes, and she and the maid returned home, where the other shoe dropped.

Her father, the doctor, pointed an angry finger at her. "You were wrong in what you did," he said. "You could ruin the druggist's business!"

"How can you say what he did was right, and what did I do wrong?" my grandmother asked.

"It may not be right," he said, "but it is the way things are." And he forbade her from doing anything like that again.

My father never forgot that story; it would bear fruit decades later in helping him empathize with those who were discriminated against. As would another anecdote about a black friend who lived next door to my dad in Virginia. The boy's father was a high-ranking officer in the Navy—in fact the first African American to be promoted to the rank of admiral. My father respected him for that. The two families had become friends.

But when a white kid called a black kid "a nigger," my father, for the first time, came face-to-face with prejudice. In time to come, he would experience it not as an observer but as a victim.

Before my dad's junior year of high school, his father was transferred to Hawaii, specifically to Oahu. Dad envisioned the typical tropical-island images—sand, surf, and palm trees. But his first impression was something different—a Filipino student holding a broken bottle was chasing a white student down the hallway. School administrators routinely brought in dogs to check lockers for pot; the dogs went crazy. Marijuana was every-where. So was racial tension.

"For the first time in my life, I experienced what it was like to be a minority," my father later wrote. Any person of non-Polynesian descent was called a f—Haole (pronounced Howlie and meaning foreigner). And, yes, the swearword was *always* included. It was a term of contempt for foreigners. Now he knew how his friends in Virginia had felt when they'd been the target of racism.

The one place he felt safe in Hawaii was church. "We were loved beyond words by the people and pastor of Wahiawa Baptist Church," he wrote.

The congregation was ethnically diverse—Filipino, Caucasian, Samoan, Hawaiian, and Japanese. To my dad, it felt like one big family. He had a decent voice and sang in the church choir. When auditions for a production of *Jesus Christ Superstar* were held, a friend suggested my dad try out. He won the lead part, which was wonderful until he learned that during the finale, where Jesus walked down the auditorium aisle, he needed to carry a cross.

It was heavy and rough-hewn. Dad was agreeable to wearing the loincloth, but, no, this was too much. It was humiliating. At the scene's end, he'd be dressed in a gold robe and climbing a ladder for the ascension scene. "I liked that part just fine," wrote my father, "but carrying a cross? Nope. Not me."

So he did what he often did in tight situations—he manipulated. He told the director it just wasn't logical to sing and carry a cross at the same time; better if he were to just sing and leave the heavy lifting, literally, to someone else.

A kid named Steve volunteered for the job. In fact, he was pumped for the opportunity. "You mean I'll actually get to carry Jesus' cross?" he said. "Mike, thanks so much."

"Hey, don't mention it," my dad answered. My father took credit for the idea, like he was doing the kid a favor. But inside he was thinking, *Are you kidding me? Who wants to carry a cross?*

Night after night, as the play ran, my father performed as the Jesus without a cross. "I loved the applause, the acclaim, the praise of the crowds," he wrote. Thousands of people showed up, and my dad belted out the grand finale and took his bows with glee.

"That," he later said, "was the picture of my Christian life. There was no taking up the cross for me. No denying myself. No true identification with Christ. No suffering or shame. Just hand me the robe, thank you, and let me take my bows."

Four

GETTING HIS WAY

:::::

In 1979, my dad was living what he thought was the dream—
tooling around Fort Worth, Texas, in his grandparents' spare
Cadillac, trying on the thought that this was what he wanted
in life. He had won a voice scholarship to Texas Christian
University. The campus was just down the street from where his
grandparents lived in Fort Worth, so he stayed in a spare room.

He had entertained thoughts of becoming a professional
singer but soon realized that was a reach, so he changed his major
to something in which he knew he could succeed—business.

He hooked up with a multilevel marketing company that
sold household products. Naturally, he was good at it. People
were drawn to my dad because he promised he could make them
lots of money and because he had boundless enthusiasm for the
job. Soon he had a hundred distributors working beneath him.

Wherever he went, whomever he met, he looked at the person, first, with this in mind: *Could they be a distributor for me?* To
him, people were tools to help him get what he wanted.

He spent the summer in San Antonio with his family, his
father having been transferred to Fort Sam Houston. There he

met a strawberry redhead named Laura Freeman, whose father was also stationed there. She would one day be my mom.

The two had a few things in common, including military fathers who had served in Vietnam. But what made their relationship work was as much their differences as their similarities, in particular how each drew on the other's strength. Mom gave my impetuous father an anchor of sorts; Dad gave my reserved mother a sense of shoot-for-the-stars excitement.

"Our relationship was a breath of fresh air in my otherwise stuffy world," he wrote. "We talked to each other about all the deep things we could imagine. I felt like I'd been underwater so long that I was about to drown, but meeting her was like coming up for air."

God would need to find a place in line. Dad moved out of his grandparents' house and into a fraternity, going to church only out of obligation. For him, God was about dos and don'ts, about religion, not a relationship. Mom, meanwhile, took her faith seriously. And walked the talk.

My father craved the faith she had. "She was everything I was not." And he wanted her to be his wife. After he graduated from TCU and she from Baylor, they were married on September 10, 1983.

They moved to Dallas, where my father went to work as an insurance underwriter, his self-confidence high and his ego large. "Mike thought he was God's gift to Chubb Insurance," said Mary Anderwald, a supervisor at the agency and later Dad's assistant. "And he convinced a lot of people of that. He wasn't short on arrogance."

He traded his and Mom's BMW for a new Mercedes. "I wanted to announce to everybody," he later wrote, "that we were the real deal."

While Dad was seeing all his dreams come to fruition, Mom wasn't so sure. She had originally resisted buying the BMW, much less the Mercedes. But my dad did his best to convince her otherwise. To understand how manipulative he could be, he treated her to a vacation week in Mexico—with the sole purpose of softening her up to say yes to the Mercedes.

"God wanted us to have this car, I was positive," he wrote. "We were the rising stars of our church. We taught a class for young marrieds. I was set to become a deacon soon. We had long ago both prayed the prayer to become Christians. This was the good life that God promised us, wasn't it?"

Again, Mom wasn't convinced. But she loved him deeply, supported him unequivocally, and prayed for him almost unceasingly. Her faith continued to deepen, and my father's remained impressive from the outside—he at least looked the part—but was empty on the inside. Just like a number of other newly married couples who attended Prestonwood Baptist Church in upscale Plano.

He loved the materialistic excess of Dallas as much as he loved cheesecake, which meant considerably. Loved that Dallas had more than twice the national average of shopping malls. Loved the way it was important to not only *have* money but to *flaunt* it.

Members of his Sunday school class would drive up to church in a new Mercedes or Lexus and show off their car to my dad.

Because he was their Sunday school teacher, he would certainly understand why they *had* to have it. And he did.

"We deserved this," he wrote. "This was our dream. This was the way we were supposed to be living, all of us who loved God."

But in time, he would come to realize that God is far more interested in our character than our comfort.

Five

MEETING MISS VELMA

::::

"Disarmingly self-righteous." Looking back, that's how my father described the 1989 model of Mike Fechner.

"He was right when he described himself like that," said Mike Buster, the executive pastor at Prestonwood. "Everyone thought he was a great spiritual leader, but internally he was not. He was a Pharisee. His heart was in worldly pleasures."

Buster became a close friend to my father and saw potential in my dad that my dad didn't see in himself. Meanwhile, Prestonwood's new senior pastor, Dr. Jack Graham, taught Dad that God wasn't our personal genie designed to meet our every materialistic desire. Graham inspired him to dig deeper into the Word of God.

Still, it was as if God needed to make use of something more dramatic to bring my father face-to-face with the "showroom" he'd really become. More precisely, some*one*. Her name was Velma Mitchell. If my father was developing a new understanding of faith and a new desire for the Word of God, Velma would offer my father a way to put his deepening faith into action.

A purpose. It was a lesson that revolutionized my father's life.

In the fall of 1989, the former mayor of Dallas was leading an initiative to bring North Dallas mentors to a place south of downtown Dallas called Bonton, a hotbed of poverty, drugs, crime, and hopelessness. My dad didn't know much about Bonton—nor, frankly, did he care—but he was intrigued by the chance to rub shoulders with the former mayor of Dallas, which might open new business opportunities. That's why my dad agreed to attend a meeting at a Bonton high school regarding outreach to the poor.

He waxed his Mercedes—a powerful person like the former mayor might notice something like that—and cruised south toward downtown Dallas. Once the freeway passed through the swanky high-rises of downtown, my father began seeing a part of the city he'd never seen before.

His world was the manicured perfection of North Dallas, the shiny skyscrapers, and the glittering Galleria Mall. But he started seeing trash along the streets, unwashed men sitting on corners and drinking from bottles, battered wood fences, scrap yards, and row after row of tiny post–World War II houses—most dingy, some boarded up.

He found the high school and locked the doors on his Mercedes, looking around to make sure nobody was eyeing it. Because of safety precautions, Dad and others had to pass through metal detectors to enter the high school. About thirty-five community and civic leaders huddled around Styrofoam coffee cups, waiting for the meeting to start.

Most were African Americans, but my father noticed a few "rich-looking white guys like me." He elbowed into the first clump of people and cracked a few jokes to lighten the mood. He was disappointed that the former Dallas mayor couldn't make it; that, of course, was the only reason he had come.

Someone called the meeting to order, and speaker after speaker took to the microphone. Toward the end of the meeting, one final speaker walked to the front. She was black and looked to be about fifteen years older than my father. She had a mass of dark curly hair and a flash of gold teeth. When she smiled, it was like the light in the room turned on. My father sensed she was a force to be reckoned with. A natural leader.

It was Velma Mitchell. When she took the microphone, the room stilled to a new level of quiet. "I was one of eleven children, and life was not easy," she said. "One day, my mama gathered us children together and gave us each a stick. 'Can you break your stick?' One by one, each child snapped their stick. Then she took eleven sticks and bunched them together. 'Can anyone break these?' None of us could. This situation in Bonton is just like our family. If we stand together, then no one can break us. But if we go out alone, we will not stand."

She paused and scanned the room, a few white faces sprinkled amid the black. "We all need to look out for one another," she said. "And if someone needs something, we need to be there for them."

My father mentally gulped. He shut off his comedian shtick. Velma spoke of hope like he'd never heard it spoken of before. She prayed like Jesus was really in the room. She basked in the anticipation of community renewal.

Then, much to my father's surprise, she sang. It was just her with a microphone. No guitar, band, or backing tape like my dad would have used. And she wasn't singing in the four-thousand-seat auditorium my father worshiped in, but in a dilapidated high school classroom in a South Dallas ghetto. But as she started to sing, it was as if the music permeated my father's very soul, unlocking the pride and arrogance that drove so many of his decisions. The melody poured out of her, dusky and soulful, and the sound filled the room with what he would describe as a strange sense of "security and guarantee."

It was an old hymn. *Be very sure, be very sure; your anchor holds and grips the Solid Rock!*

It was as if the song were a sort of auditory window cleaner to help him see himself more clearly than before. As if each word she sang wiped off a smudge of pride that my father's life of privilege had built up.

When she finished and sat down, the people sat in stunned silence for a moment, as if realizing they'd been in the presence of something special. Then a single voice uttered a loud "Amen!" and all broke loose with clapping. Nobody clapped more feverishly than my father.

He was a white, wealthy, family man from North Dallas. She was a poor, black, single mom from South Dallas. But she had something—a peace of mind, a contentment, an assurance—that he did not. And he wanted it badly.

This may sound strange, given how our culture neatly divides winners and losers by income, status, and the like, but in a world of haves and have-nots, my father realized in that moment that all the stuff of appearance meant absolutely squat. Nothing. Zero.

Velma was a "have"; my father, he realized, was a "have not."

The meeting ended, and people scattered. As he walked to his car, something happened that was either a comment on the materialistic world on which he'd built his life, a premonition of where that life was headed, or a deft touch from a God with a wonderful sense of humor. Perhaps all three.

A dog lifted its leg on a tire of his $50,000 Mercedes and welcomed him to the neighborhood.

Six

A PARTNERSHIP BORN

:::::

My father's past and Velma's past couldn't have been more different. His, of course, was an upbringing of privilege, hers an upbringing of pain. His family members employed African-American maids. Her family members *were*, in essence, those maids.

She was born in 1947, the seventh of eleven children. Her daddy was a sharecropper and died when Velma was young. Her mama did everything she could to help the family survive. They lived in a shack on a white man's farm and grew their own food.

The white man didn't allow the African-American kids whose parents grew his crops to attend school. He thought it was too distracting during planting and harvest seasons. Velma's mama said, "Enough," and moved her children to Tyler, Texas, where they could get an education. Velma was nine years old before she ever set foot in a schoolhouse.

Like my father, Velma prayed to accept Jesus when she was young. However, when she grew up and moved to Dallas, she began hanging with the wrong crowd. She smoked and drank and did drugs. She married at twenty-one, and a few years later, she and her husband had a son named Romon. Her husband lashed Velma with verbal and physical abuse. One day, she got fed up and told him to leave. He threatened to kill her and chased her, but she escaped with Romon. She went to the police and got a restraining order and, ultimately, a legal separation.

Later, at the funeral for Velma's nephew—killed in a drive-by shooting—the pastor spoke about the love and forgiveness of Jesus. He invited anyone who was backsliding or not saved to stand. Velma stood up and surrendered her life to Jesus.

The drug habit ended. Her life underwent a transformation. She had known despair and darkness. Now she delved deeply into the Word of God. Velma began to pray and fast regularly, and she sensed God working strongly in her life.

By the time she met my father in 1989, Velma still had little in the way of money or possessions. She lived in Turner Courts, a public housing project in Bonton. Her neighbor was a drug dealer. A house of prostitution drew a brisk business across the street. Gunfire and police sirens shattered the night. But what Velma lacked in the way of the world's riches, she made up with faith.

That's what drew my father to her. My dad had lived an easy life and yet was still a fledgling in his faith. Velma, on the other hand, had lived a horrific life but stuck to God like Velcro.

"I would quickly come to see that Velma had everything I ever truly wanted in life," my father wrote. "Not money, no. But inner serenity. Abundant hope. Even the respect of the community. I needed to be part of her bundle of sticks. I needed to align myself and my family with the God of her faith so that when hard times came, I would not be snapped."

In November 1989, a few months after my father heard Velma

sing, she and Romon showed up at Prestonwood for a "To Dallas with Love" outreach event at which Jack Graham was speaking. My mother and father also attended the event.

It was winter. It was cold. And nothing against Graham, but at the moment, Velma was more interested in a coat for her son than about any sort of spiritual sustenance. She and Romon were greeted warmly upon arrival. She enjoyed Graham's message; "there was something special about him," she later said.

But during the prayer, she had to be honest with God: *Please, Lord, I'm so worried about my boy this winter. If there is any way a coat could be found for him, I would be so grateful. I don't have the money, but I trust you to provide what I cannot. Amen. Oh, and the school pictures. Twenty dollars that we don't have. I don't mean to be a burden, but if that's possible . . .*

At the time, she had fifteen cents to her name. That night, after returning home, Velma decided there was only one thing to do: fast with the expectation that God would meet her and Romon's needs. On the night after the Prestonwood event, she was in prayer at their home when she heard a light knock on the door.

Her heart began thumping. Nobody knocked on her door at night. *Drug runners after her teenage son? Cops? What?* She timidly opened the door. There stood a couple about thirty years old. Well-dressed. Nervous-looking. And white. Her eyes swept the neighborhood, left and right. It wasn't safe for two white people to be in this neighborhood at night.

"Hello," said the man—not my father, by the way. "We're from Prestonwood Baptist. We saw you last night."

Velma nervously ushered them inside.

"We were praying for the people who came to the event last night," said the young woman, "and God impressed on our hearts that you needed something for your son."

She pulled out a coat for Romon. Velma's jaw dropped. Romon came to the door, saw the coat, and smiled big. He tried on the coat. Perfect fit. Velma turned to hug the woman. At the hug's end, the visitor pressed something into the woman's hand—a $20 bill.

As he heard of this act of kindness, my father began to learn that life wasn't about getting; it was about giving. This was an intriguing concept, though not one he was particularly familiar with.

Seven

REACHING OUT

:::::

At the time my father met Velma Mitchell, he was twenty-eight, she forty-two. Soon my dad and mom got involved in a mentoring program of which Velma was a part. The idea was to help single mothers in South Dallas get their GEDs, and Velma helped organize the program.

In the months to come, a friendly game of relational ping-pong began as the two got to know and trust each other. Dad invited Velma to Prestonwood Baptist Church. She accepted and came, though it was a cultural clash of epic proportions—her attending a church with thousands of other people, most of them white.

She invited my dad and my mom to a family reunion. They accepted and came. They were the only white people in the bunch, and the gathering took place in the kind of sketchy neighborhood they had never seen before meeting Velma.

Dad started to get to know Velma's teenage son, Romon. (I was only a couple of years old at the time.) The boy had never had a father figure in his life, and like most others in such circumstances, he was learning his lessons on the street—some the hard way. He'd grown distant from Velma. Sullen. Secretive.

Though my father found him quiet, respectful, and open to learning. "Precious," he wrote.

Velma asked Dad to join her on the board of an urban renewal organization called the STEP Foundation. He accepted.

Bonton was the most dangerous place in Dallas, but Velma was intent on changing that. Gunfire from gang warfare peppered the night. Mothers and children would sleep on the floor in case stray bullets came through the windows. And mothers of boys like Romon found themselves attending far too many funerals, weeping for young men who'd died in drive-by shootings, never having had much of a chance to escape the hood and the dangers therein.

When my father first saw Velma and Romon's house, he had one of his crews come to install a security alarm system. The ramshackle house was a break-in waiting to happen—doors that could practically be blown down, holes in the walls, cracks around the doors and windows.

But as Dad came alongside Velma to teach her about protecting herself and her son, she came alongside him with deeper stuff. God stuff. "Velma began to teach me one of the greatest secrets of her life," he wrote. It was about where our real security needs to ultimately rest.

"Unless the Lord watches over my house," she told him, "you and your home security company are watching in vain."

Velma became a catalyst to both deepen and broaden my father's faith. Deepen it, because seeing someone so economically destitute and spiritually full made him realize how wrong he'd been in believing that faith and material blessings went hand in hand. And broaden it, because Bonton represented a world he'd never paid a lick of attention to—and now it seemed full of possibilities to him, a chance for him to be salt and light far from the trappings of wealth and privilege.

He wondered what the two of them might do for Bonton if they worked together. Quietly, she wondered the same thing. Dad had long been an opportunist. Now, Velma Mitchell and Bonton provided an opportunity that was not only more challenging than anything he'd ever tackled, but one with deeper promise. This wasn't some way to become wealthier; he was already close to being a millionaire. No, it was something real instead of fool's gold.

For years, Velma had been toiling in the shadows, trying to help save a place that had become something of a war zone. Suddenly, she had someone who caught a vision to better this place and had ideas of his own about how that might be done. An advocate. An encourager.

As Dad deepened his relationship with Velma and Romon, my mom started appreciating how this woman of simple faith had unleashed a whole new side to Dad's dormant faith. My dad and Velma's relationship was part mentor/student, part brother and sister in Christ, and part simply friends. I was pretty small at the time, about three or four, but Velma and I quickly developed a good connection too.

Slowly but surely, Dad and Velma were bridging each other's worlds. With God as their common link, who knew what they could accomplish?

Eight

TRADING
PERSPECTIVES

:::::

Velma was like a gnarled tree growing out of a rock; she hadn't had the best upbringing, and she wasn't living in a place that offered much nourishment—but somehow, between her faith in God and her deep-rooted stubbornness, she was going to grow. She was going to change whatever she could change in Bonton.

She helped implement a GED program through the Mary Crowley Academy, which needed twenty-five students to stay open. She would knock on door after door in the Bonton neighborhood, all but begging residents to complete their education.

She prayed for the students by name. "If they did not come to school, I went to their houses and woke them up and got them there," she said. "If they didn't answer the doors, I pushed the mailbox lid open. If I smelled food, I yelled, 'Come to school! Come to school!'" Twenty-six students signed up that semester. Twenty-six finished.

Together, beginning with a simple Bible study that she and

my dad co-led, the two of them talked of forging a ministry that would be mutually beneficial to the folks in Bonton and to the folks at Prestonwood. The Plano people, my dad reasoned, could broaden their perspectives and realize that only a half hour from their opulent homes lived people whose problems went far beyond fighting rush-hour traffic.

Meanwhile, the Bonton people could broaden their perspective too and realize that people with money can still have hearts and faith and compassion. Like Velma's "sticks in a bunch," they could all—regardless of where they lived—be better together than they might be apart.

Thus would my father go to Bonton every week to spend time with the people, ask them what they needed, and start dreaming about what might come of this new partnership. And thus would Velma come to Prestonwood as part of a recruiting effort in which she approached dozens of Dallas churches, trying to get them to send volunteers to help in her community.

As she did so, Velma found an acceptance that surprised her. She'd been attending her brother's congregation, an all-black church near Bonton, but she'd felt "beat down there." And though she'd considered helping with his ministry, her brother moved away.

She had to drive forty minutes to get to Prestonwood, longer than it took tollway travelers, because she couldn't afford the tolls and faced a bunch of traffic signals. Soon, she and Romon started riding the bus. In the fall of 1991, one Sunday morning at Prestonwood, she asked my dad, "Mike, can I join the church?"

"Well, of course," he said. When she went to the front of the church to indicate her desire to become a member, my father went with her.

The next day, she worried how people at STEP would react to her decision. Would they see it as a betrayal? A selling out to whitey? Not at all—but for reasons you might not expect. "Do you know what this means for our organization? That is one of the largest churches in Dallas. This will definitely help out our ministry. Mike goes there."

Velma saw things differently. "I was looking for Jesus," she said, "but they were looking for money."

When some of Velma's non-work friends heard she and Romon had joined Prestonwood in upscale Plano, they thought she'd gone nuts. She didn't care. The church had accepted her.

"It was like God was releasing me to go to Prestonwood," she said. "I kept prayin' to God, *I thought you would let me work in ministry with my brother.* God finally got through to me that you *are* working in ministry with your brother. Your brother *Mike.*"

When people try to bridge cultural gaps, awkward situations are inevitable. My father couldn't begin to speak the language, look the look, or walk the walk of an African-American man in Bonton; he didn't even try. At times, he got some smirks—the guy had seemingly been born with a Ralph Lauren polo shirt affixed to him. And when people saw his Mercedes, they figured his arrival in the neighborhood must have something to do with drugs. But people couldn't dispute something that transcended his appearance—his heart.

He genuinely cared about this community. Meanwhile, Velma bonded with the people at Prestonwood, even though she had her moments. She was invited to speak to a group of Prestonwood women about a project to benefit Bonton children, and at Dad's urging, she accepted. The talk was to be held in a plush North Dallas house. She had never been in a house so nice, a spiral staircase anchoring the entryway. She arrived early, wearing a black blouse and skirt. Her host showed her where she would be speaking and invited her to make herself at home.

Velma gravitated to the kitchen, which interested her because she loved to cook. Other women started arriving and nibbling on food, drinking coffee, sipping tea, and, not incidentally, asking Velma for refills. Handing plates and cups to her. *Thanking her for her help.*

They had naturally assumed that since she was black and in a plush North Dallas house, she must be the maid. Velma didn't feel comfortable saying she was not.

Later, when she was introduced as the speaker, the women were stunned and embarrassed at their assumptions. But the next year, after they heard about a tragedy that had befallen Velma, those same Prestonwood folks stepped up to encourage and support the woman they'd mistaken for the maid.

The tragedy involved Romon, her only child.

Nine

LOOKING AT LIFE FROM BOTH SIDES NOW

::::

By Christmas, a few months after he had met Velma, my father's life was changing fast, though he'd hardly done an about-face. This new relationship with Velma and Romon had opened him to the realness of the gospel, but when cast as a gold-caped king with a solo for Prestonwood's extravagant Christmas musical, he said, "I still greatly loved the applause."

At his invitation, Velma and Romon attended one of the performances. Afterward, Romon, then fourteen, was wide-eyed at seeing my dad up close, dressed as a king. "Mama," he said breathlessly, within earshot of my father, "Uncle Mike is the gold king!"

At Easter, he was cast as Judas and sold out Jesus for thirty pieces of silver. "I found it surprisingly easy to identify with the character of Judas," he wrote. "Even the choir director commented on how easily I became the betrayer. The awakening was happening now, for sure. I was realizing how much my life revolved around bringing *me* glory. I had faith in Jesus, but my faith was still transactional, not transformational. I liked Jesus because of what he could do for *me*."

But, slowly, that perspective was changing. The once-indifferent Bible reader was now digging deeply into the Word—as he described it, "like a parched man in the desert receiving a pitcher of ice-cold water. This became a season of repentance for me, of taking the Word of God and combining it with prayer and sensing for the first time the incredible power and richness of knowing God. I came alive inside, but the focus wasn't on me this time; it was on knowing God."

Meanwhile after working with Velma, he began realizing how skewed his vision of the world had been, how easily he took for granted the privileges he had. "In Dallas, if you didn't have money, then injustices abounded," he wrote. "It was hard to get a check cashed. If you had problems, you needed to navigate an endless string of bureaucratic government agencies. It was even difficult to go to a grocery store. If you lived in Bonton and couldn't afford a car, it meant you rode the bus. You could get snacks, beer, and cigarettes at the corner marts in Bonton, but if you wanted real food—something besides junk food—it would require a three-hour bus ride there and back. So it was easier to eat junk."

My father taught a Bible study in the apartment of a resident who lived in the Turner Courts housing development. It was winter. A rat was stuck in the house's heating ducts, and whenever the owner of the house turned on the heat, the house smelled like a charred rodent—one of those things you needn't worry about in Plano.

But my dad fell in love with the people participating in the study. He couldn't believe their graciousness, their warmth, their sense of community. He and Velma had only been leading the group for a month when Velma informed them it was my father's birthday. "We need to celebrate," she said.

Now, remember, my father was head of a business that would soon make him a millionaire. All of the people in this room were on public assistance. But they lavished him with a cake. And gifts. Not just any gifts, but stuff they'd heard him say he liked. One woman bought him an expensive French candle; weird, I know, but my dad loved such candles.

"I sat there and cried," he wrote. "I knew people all over the city of Dallas by then, many of whom were extremely wealthy. None of them had bought me gifts. Yet these poverty-stricken residents of Bonton had bought me gifts—and extremely thoughtful gifts at that."

Weeks later, Velma called Dad at work. A black woman who worked with Velma at STEP was having difficulty getting a check cashed. Could my father help?

He met them at a large downtown bank and expected there would be no problem. He was wrong. The teller was rude. "She made my new friend feel like a fool for supposing the bank would cash her check with no account, even with my guaranty," he wrote. "This angered me greatly."

Long story short, he finally found a vice president, and after he dropped the name of a high-ranking executive he knew, the VP instructed the teller to cash the check immediately. But the whole process had taken nearly an hour. And my father believed it was because of a subtle bias that bank employees had against a couple of poor black women.

My father began learning an important lesson about himself: Just like the Pharisees, who used rules and traditions as reasons to not follow Jesus—as in John 9 regarding working on the Sabbath—he had hardened his heart to loving people as God calls his disciples to. Instead, he had hidden behind being a great rule follower. Now, he was beginning to see that rules weren't the point. He was beginning to see how institutions couldn't really help an individual; only people could help people.

If the bank incident embarrassed Velma and her friend, it did something else too: It made her realize that Mike Fechner had her back. "Velma left the bank that day, knowing she wasn't the only one who could stand up and fight if needed," wrote my father. "That day, we realized we were both fighters—her against injustice in her community and me against injustices in the system."

Ten

THE PHONE CALL

:::::

My father came to Velma and asked permission to mentor Romon. She eagerly gave her OK. My dad could model for her son what a godly man was all about—something the boy had never had.

Romon was a wiry, good-looking kid with an athletic build and his mother's smile. Winsome. Upbeat. Gracious. Soft-spoken but exuding a quiet confidence. My father would take Romon out to eat and listen to him, hearing what was on his heart. This was particularly significant because most white guys in that situation would come in with a sense of arrogance about how much they knew and the other guy didn't.

Romon was surprised that my father wanted to spend time with him. With few exceptions, most men wanted Romon to run drugs for them. To use him for their advantage, not to help him for his own sake. On the other hand, my father, in his relationship with Romon, experienced something he'd never experienced before. "My relationship with Romon was the first one in my life that wasn't about me getting what I needed," he wrote, "but about what Romon needed."

They talked about everything—school, family, dating, the father Romon had never known. I was only four years old at the time; I hardly remember Romon. But my father loved him dearly. "He was such a wonderful young man," he wrote.

Months turned into a year; one year into two. The two kept meeting. In some ways, Romon became like a second son to him. At times, Romon was making poor choices in life, but my dad had grown to understand the culture of which he was part—a culture that did little or nothing to encourage smart choices.

The chasm separating the culture of Plano from that of Bonton was wide. If my father talked to a teen at Prestonwood Baptist Church, he might ask about which university he planned to attend, what his hopes and dreams were. In Bonton, that didn't work. "If I asked Romon his hopes and dreams for the future, he'd give me a blank stare," he wrote. "Students his age were just trying to live. Most of his peers felt lucky if they reached twenty-one and hadn't been killed or thrown in jail. Oh, they might want a house, a job, to get a little place of their own to stay. But it was a totally different paradigm. It wasn't a question of ambition. It was a problem of no opportunity, real or perceived."

By the time Romon had turned seventeen, he had fathered a baby girl. My dad encouraged him to marry the girl's mother, young as they were, so they could provide a stable household for their son. And he did. He and his young wife moved in with Velma, and together they began raising their daughter, Shayla, and would soon have a nephew joining them too.

Eleven months later, another baby was born—a boy. They

named him Romon Jr. "They were both beautiful children," my father wrote. "Velma's grandchildren." Velma was only forty-five herself.

My mom and dad prayed and prayed for Velma and her growing family. Naturally, there was talk in the hood that my father was somehow out to exploit Romon; why else would a rich guy in a Mercedes be taking a black teenager out to Red Lobster week after week? But after months of Mike investing in the young man, Velma asked her son about him one evening.

"Mama," Romon said, "he's real. Mike is cool. Mike understands."

Hearing that later, my father was humbled. "They saw in me what I didn't even see in myself," he wrote. "God was building a beautiful bridge. God knit Velma's family's and my family's hearts together through her son."

It was Labor Day weekend 1992. It had been a particularly tough stretch for Velma and her family. Her mother had recently died. Two small children and a nephew of hers lived with Velma and Romon and his wife in a tiny house; the stress was taking its toll. Romon seemed a touch more uptight than usual. His wife was gone. So, knowing her son well, Velma left to get him something she knew he'd love—ice cream.

When she returned, he was gone. Her nephew was watching Shayla and Romon Jr. He said Romon told him he'd be back soon. But "soon" came and went. Velma fed and bathed the kids, put them to bed, and sang them to sleep.

Toward daybreak, a knock on the front door jolted Velma.

"Police!" a voice yelled.

Velma checked through the tiny window and saw a plain-clothes officer.

She grudgingly opened the door, wanting the truth and *not* wanting the truth. "Do you have a son named Romon Mitchell?" he asked.

"Yes," Velma said. "Is he in trouble?"

"No," said the detective, and then he paused and looked down. "Romon Mitchell is dead."

He had been killed in a drive-by shooting.

Eleven

A STIRRING
OF THE SOUL

:::::

The phone rang at our house in the early hours of the morning. When my mother realized it was a weeping Velma, she gave the phone to Dad.

"Mike," said Velma, "there's a man here, and I'm thinking he's gotta be crazy. He's telling me my baby's gone. My baby's dead!"

My father, still in bed, tried to make sense of what she was saying but couldn't. "I'm on my way," he said.

By the time he arrived, Velma's yard was packed with cars. She'd phoned a relative, and word had spread. First, African-American folks, then, oddly, a white guy from Plano. And later, others from Plano—people who knew Velma and Romon. More than one hundred people from Prestonwood arrived to show their support for Velma Mitchell. I'm not sure my father was ever prouder of Prestonwood.

"I'm so sorry," he said to Velma, kneeling down in front of the woman sitting in a chair, motionless.

Hugs. Wet faces. Red eyes. Velma asked my father about funeral arrangements. She had no insurance on her son.

"That's not for you to worry about," my dad said. He talked to some of his friends; the funeral would be paid for.

"It was the strangest mix of days," my father remembered. "It was like a worship service was held in Velma's front room. People came by and prayed and sang songs and wept with her. People spoke openly about God to anyone who came by." Five people professed faith in Jesus.

Even as seventeen-month-old Shayla asked for her daddy every so often, something was happening, as if Romon's death had unleashed God's power in a new and amazing way.

"It was like a dam had broke," recalled my father, "and the love and care of the community flooded out in a huge wave of support."

Much of that support came from Prestonwood people. Velma's tired appliances were replaced by new appliances. Her house was painted, yard landscaped, lawn mowed. No charge. It was as if these brothers and sisters in Christ were saying, *We can't bring Romon back, but we can remind you that you, Velma, are loved.*

Jack Graham, who had come to support Velma after Romon was killed, hosted a radio show and invited Velma to speak of the incident. She did so, and for weeks afterward, she received letters from across the country, some containing checks. Strangers wrote to say they were praying for her. Meals kept arriving, many provided by the women in that North Dallas Bible study who had once mistaken her for the maid. Now they were serving her.

When Velma was invited to speak at a Prestonwood retreat

near Austin, she wasn't sure how she would get there. Mary Anderwald, a Prestonwood member, volunteered to take her. "She loves people and is very genuine," said Velma. "That particular time Mary served me as if I was one of the most important people in the world, and I just couldn't believe it. I'm like, 'God, there is no reason for her to be this nice to me. I don't know her, she don't know me.' But finally I got it through this thick head of mine that when you love Jesus, you love Jesus' people."

One day, Velma turned to my father. "Now I know why God brought me to Prestonwood," she said. "That church family loved me in ways I never dreamed."

And to some degree, my father better understood why God had brought him to Bonton. While he appeared strong and composed for Velma, once home he wept for his adopted son, Romon. "I wanted to take the pain away from Velma, but that was something only the Lord could do," he wrote. "All I could do was pray and ask God to show me what to do."

Over the next few weeks and months, he could not get over the death of Romon. The senselessness of it. The hopelessness that so many of these young men felt. The callousness of a world in which life was considered so cheap that someone would start blasting away without caring whom he hit.

"The murder of Romon struck me like a bolt of lightning because of the injustice and inequity of it all," wrote my father, who'd already seen how people in poor areas such as Bonton could be exploited. He watched people in the projects get charged thirty dollars a month to rent an old washer or dryer and then, when it broke down, be told, "Sorry, no warranty."

Dad was confronted with a paradox: God's kingdom is built on justice and love. If he was a child of the King, shouldn't he be fighting for these things, especially when injustice and hate existed in his own backyard?

"I wanted the whole system to change, the whole culture that had sowed the seeds of destruction that led to Romon's death," he wrote. "I didn't want anybody to grow up without a father ever again. I didn't want any young man not to have a hope and a future. The death of Romon Mitchell was a wake-up call to my soul."

Twelve

SMALL MIRACLES

::::

My father and Velma ramped up their vision to take back Bonton from the drug dealers and pimps and give hope to the hopeless. As part of the STEP Foundation, they kicked around the idea of forming a faith-based offspring. The two imagined jobless people finding work, sick people getting well, hopeless people finding faith. They envisioned a spiritual element to the work that would suggest God's kingdom is about restoring life—not just spiritually, but physically, emotionally, and socioeconomically. And not in some fuzzy "someday" in the future, but now.

They envisioned an unofficial relationship between Prestonwood people and Bonton. People helping people. My father remained convinced that whatever bridge they were building wouldn't be one-way, but two-way. Already, he'd seen his faith revolutionized by getting to know people so different from him. Could God rejuvenate others, like God had rejuvenated him?

To seal their plan, the two of them, as my father wrote, "prayed through the streets of Bonton." This wasn't going to be any far-off dream you wait on for five years to get funding. It was going to be like riding a bicycle and putting it together at the same time—with God supplying the needs however he saw fit.

Velma had a certain respect in Bonton, especially with young men, some of whom considered her their mother. "I watched Velma love these young men," he wrote. "Her maternal instincts never stopped."

One of those young men, a guy named Lavar, had earned a college scholarship, but nobody would hire him, and he needed money. Velma appealed to my father. Dad interviewed Lavar, during which time the young man said he'd like to go to church but didn't have nice enough shoes.

My father's response was symbolic of the man he was beginning to become. He prayed with Lavar. He vowed to help him find a job, a promise he later made good on. And, finally, he did something I can't imagine the old Mike Fechner doing: He took off his shoes and handed them to the young man.

In December 1993—I was five years old, my younger brother Daniel, two—my father invited Velma, her daughter-in-law, and her two grandchildren to join our extended family in San Antonio for Christmas. From the outside, her joining the family would be cathartic for a woman who had lost her son sixteen months earlier.

My grandparents were initially hesitant to have Velma's family join them, not because she was black but because, traditionally, Christmas was family time and, well, she wasn't family. But they gave in to my father's request.

The Fechners gave her gifts, something she never expected. But in the end, our family believed we, not she, were the true beneficiaries. "The Lord was rocking and breaking things in our family that needed to be broken for his purpose," said my father, whose ninety-year-old grandmother—my great-grandmother—initially thought Velma was her maid and called her "girl."

By the end of the celebration, she was holding Velma's hand and welcoming the "godly warmth" that she had brought to the occasion. Lessons had been learned—by our family and by Velma.

"I had no idea that God wasn't sending me so I could be helped by the Fechners but so *I* could help the Fechners," said Velma. "How little we know what God's total purposes are—beyond our understanding and imaginations."

But she and her new brother, Mike, would ultimately find out.

It would not be a smooth, straight path. Nor would their inspiration always come in ways they might have expected.

But, then, Velma's visit to San Antonio had already proven to be a catalyst for a miracle that would bear fruit years later in the same house where she had spent Christmas. My grandparents not only began to develop a heart for those less fortunate, but they put it into practice. They soon opened their home to a black teenage brother and sister who otherwise would have been homeless. My grandparents poured their hearts into these kids, helping them with schoolwork, advocating to their teachers, and, in essence, saying, *You're family.*

I like to look at that time with Velma as God seeding a Christmas miracle that would later sprout grandly. And if it were the first step in Velma and my father's plan to bridge cultural gaps, it would not be the last.

Thirteen

THE DECISION

:::::

One day, after coleading a Bible study, my father and Velma headed out for lunch, not an uncommon act for them.

"What would you like?" Dad asked.

"I'm not eating, Mike," she said.

My father figured this was about money, or lack thereof.

"I'm happy to pay," he said.

"That's not it," she said. "I'm fasting."

Fasting, she told him, lessens our dependence on self and deepens our dependence on God. She was talking, of course, to a certified junk-food junkie. But she pulled out her Bible and convinced Dad that fasting was pleasing to God.

So my dad began to fast. It was just one of the many things that mirrored the change in his life. Another was prayer. As he saw Velma pray with such great expectation, he was now taking it more seriously than ever. He approached it, not as the daily obligation of, say, teeth brushing, but of listening to the heart of God. It wasn't about asking for stuff. It was about "getting God," as his friend Dr. Bob Bakke liked to say. Bakke had served as the national chairman of the Global Day of Prayer, and my father learned much about prayer from him.

He thought it was interesting that Dr. Bakke had not learned to pray in seminary or by reading a book on prayer. Instead, he said he learned to pray fervently and effectually "by praying with some dear African-American women in a downtown New York prayer revival meeting." As he heard them pray, Bakke said, "God, I do not know how to pray as they pray. I long to pray like this."

As did my father.

It was as if Velma's life had opened his eyes partway to new possibilities and perspectives—and Romon's death opened them the rest of the way.

He found this new perspective totally freeing. And absolutely frightening.

My father struggled with this challenge of becoming someone new. He had spent nearly three decades essentially living for himself. Now God seemed to be saying, *Live for others. Live for me. Be someone else.*

And yet Dad liked part of the old Mike. He liked to walk into church and imagine people thinking, *There goes a successful guy.* He wouldn't get much of that from Bonton. Instead, he might get mugged.

God seemed to be saying, *You've embraced me intellectually. You've served me. But now do more: Follow me. Really follow me, Mike, into the unknown.*

My dad loved to take risks, but this one wasn't about having the courage to start a business or lovingly confront someone about something in their life that needed fixing. This was *his* life. This was about letting go of that life and giving God complete control.

God seemed to be saying, *Trust me with your future.*

And yet, until now, Dad was a little like the person in that well-known faith story about the daredevil preparing to bicycle on a tightrope across Niagara Falls.

"How many of you believe I can do this?" he asked the throng of people. Fists pumped. People cheered. "Go! Go! Go!" they yelled.

"Wonderful!" the daredevil said. "Now I need a volunteer to ride on back of the bike. Who'd like to join me?"

Not a single hand rose into the air. Members of the crowd stood as silent as statues.

Likewise, intellectually, my father seemed poised to make a major life change, and yet what did that even look like? Where was God leading him?

Months passed. He could think of little else other than this nagging sense that God was calling him to something new. But to what, specifically?

He would be driving to work and wonder, *Is this all there is? Selling security alarms? Making money? Making more money? Buying stuff? Buying more stuff?*

He would be in Bonton and find himself strangely drawn to the place, liking it despite its darker side.

He would be praying when he sensed God was daring him to take a deeper look at his life and try to answer the question, *Couldn't I be more for your kingdom?*

For the first time, he was realizing that God wanted so much more from him than he'd been willing to give. That what God really wanted was for him to develop a hardscrabble faith like Velma's.

"My whole outlook gradually shifted," he wrote. "When it came to making money, everything I'd hoped and dreamed and prayed for had come to pass." The scheduling board at his company was packed. His phone would ring with someone wanting to talk business, the kind of call he used to see as a fat pitch he could rip over the left-field wall for a financial homer. Now, he waved in a pinch hitter by forwarding such calls to someone else.

"I had no heart to run my business anymore, to make a ton of money, or to buy a bunch of nice stuff," he wrote.

He looked inside himself and discovered what he called a "subconscious theology of comfort." While he lived morally and gave generously, he never went so far as to upset his cozy lifestyle.

Now, with a new perspective, he crunched some numbers. People in his Plano zip code area had four times the average annual income of the people in Bonton, but the people in Bonton gave triple the percent of their income to the poor compared to their wealthier counterparts.

He examined his faith and found what he termed "cafeteria-style Christianity." He was taking dessert but not eating the vegetables and nutrients his body needed to grow. "I was," he wrote, "a man with an anemic faith."

He found himself spending less time at work and more time

in Bonton. He would disciple families, volunteer in the schools, and find excuses just so he could meet new people.

My dad was like the dry bones in the valley that Ezekiel 37 refers to. Over the last several years, it was as if God had begun rattling those dry bones, methodically adding the sinew, flesh, and skin to his body. All that remained was to add breath. And that's exactly what happened next.

In February 1994, Dr. Joseph Stowell, president of Moody Bible Institute in Chicago, spoke at Prestonwood. "What are you holding on to that's not allowing you to do all that God wants you to do?" he asked. "God wants you to lay it down."

My father was in the choir loft, and when he heard those words, he thought one thing, and one thing only: *I need to sell my business.*

It was a crazy thought. At age thirty-three, he was just vain enough to know he'd recently become an official millionaire. And clearly, there was far more money where that came from. But God seemed to be whispering the words of Mark 10:21: "Go, sell everything you have and give to the poor, and you will have treasure . . ."

Here and there, people left their seats, headed for aisles, and made their way to the front of the church. My father was one of them. That night, he bowed before the Lord in humble obedience. If, as a child, he had professed a faith in Christ, now, with more knowledge and a more pliable heart, he was saying, *Jesus, I am yours. Use me how you wish.*

My folks decided to do just that. They had prayed long and

hard, concluding that God was directing them to sell the business. But there were two snags. Dad's father, Ruben, was a part-owner; if he didn't like the idea, things could get complicated. My dad contacted him. Strangely enough, he'd been thinking the same thing.

Snag Two: When Dad put the business on the sales block, he figured it might take months, if not years, to sell. Instead, the business sold within weeks.

Ready or not, Dad's new life was about to begin.

Fourteen

THE GREAT GIVEAWAY

My once-selfish father was suddenly Scrooge on Christmas morning. It started innocently enough, with relatively small amounts. Five thousand here, twenty-five thousand there, most of it going to the STEP Foundation.

"The second one hundred thousand was even easier," he wrote. "My heart was set free. It was joyous to give it away when at one time it meant so much. I couldn't wait to see a need and give."

The "old Mike" would have parted with a dollar bill as if it were the rope in a tug-of-war contest—only with great reluctance. *Mine, mine, mine!* It wasn't in his nature to give. "But," he wrote, "I couldn't help but notice when faced with a need that the strings of my heart now reverberated in new ways."

He supplemented his giving of money with giving of even more time to people in Bonton. He found himself spending more time in South Dallas than North Dallas. "I loved to be down there," he wrote. "I felt *life*. There was authenticity, community, relationships. Although a raw place, what with the gunfire at night."

He volunteered on boards whose organizations helped the poor. He worked more closely with STEP. Led Bible studies. Joined prayer walks through impoverished neighborhoods. Traveled to New York to visit inner-city ministries. And as he did so, my father began seeing others not through his own eyes but through the eyes of Christ.

"Often we let the conditions of the urban centers go unchanged because we do not live there," he wrote. "We reason, *Why should that be our burden? Why should we care for the loss of children being shot and children becoming drug addicts because they are fatherless? Is it our responsibility to be father and mother to the parentless?* The undeniable answer God was speaking into my heart was *yes.*"

Even when he used his "privilege" to, say, convince a bank vice president to cash Velma's friend's check, he understood the unfairness of the racial inequalities. "Rules bend for white guys in suits," he wrote. "Rules remain firm for older black women with tiny paychecks. In short, I found that the view from the bottom stinks."

Later, he likened this phase of his life to the apostle Paul's years in the wilderness. Dad had no job. He had no clear idea of what he was going to do next. So, yes, in some ways he was wandering. "All I knew was that my old way of life didn't work out as I'd hoped it would. Yes, it made me a 'somebody,' but the somebody I became was a somebody I didn't like. I felt no peace inside. I felt no sense of purpose. I needed to separate myself from my previous dreams so I could hear clearly the voice of God through the Bible and the power of the Holy Spirit."

One day, my father, in the back of his Bible, started jotting down different options for ministries, almost with stream-of-consciousness thinking. He enjoyed working with young people. He liked to sing. He had great respect for Campus Crusade for Christ. Those were possibilities. A dozen opportunities became two dozen. When finished, he had written down thirty possibilities. Despite his work with Velma and despite his new love for Bonton, "working in the inner city" was at the very bottom of the list.

Strange. He already had a foot in the inner city. Already had a partner in whatever mad scheme he and Velma were devising. Why was he so timid about jumping in with both feet? It was as if he were in that crowd at Niagara Falls, happy to cheer on the guy on the tightrope but not interested in volunteering himself. It would be far more comfortable to do something he already knew how to do, such as sing.

He prayed on it. Thought on it. *Maybe comfort shouldn't be the key component of this choice,* he wondered. After all, where was the faith in comfort? Wasn't that the problem with him and a lot of other Christians? They didn't take the *courageous* route but the *comfortable* route.

So in 1995, he and Velma did it—founded H.I.S. (Hope in Salvation) BridgeBuilders. Under the umbrella of STEP, it would be a ministry devoted to restoring urban communities by addressing the needs of individuals and their neighborhoods, devoted to building a bridge between the haves and have-nots, understanding that their needs were the same—a foundation in Christ—even if their lives were dramatically different.

To turn Bonton around, they needed people pulling together for a common cause. People trusting each other.

The irony of H.I.S. BridgeBuilders' early years? The new organization rose out of the ashes of betrayal.

My father had given hundreds of thousands of dollars to STEP, the umbrella organization under which BridgeBuilders operated. It was the major reason the Fechner bank account was dropping toward empty.

Then something started smelling fishy. Mom, who did the books for the new ministry, started realizing that things weren't adding up—literally and figuratively. Sure enough, some poking around soon brought to light that one of the executives of the foundation was betraying my parents, Velma, and BridgeBuilders. My father felt like the person had taken the money right from Dad's pocket and stuffed it in his own.

When he learned what was happening, my dad burst into tears. It wasn't just the loss of money; it was the deceit behind it that bothered him most.

"Mike had given all his money, just laid it up on the altar—and he was doing it for the poor," said Velma, "and now someone was trying to take him down with all the might they had."

That did it. BridgeBuilders needed to go it alone, my father decided. With his personal coffers all but dry, he made a desperate phone call from a youth camp where he'd been speaking, begging two men he knew for $12,000 to keep the ministry going. Amid a whirl of tears on all ends of the three-way conversation, the two pledged the money. But because of the split, the organization had no offices, no partners in the city, and little creative energy.

Regardless, Velma said she was quitting the STEP organization and going to work with my father, even though BridgeBuilders had nothing to pay her.

When my father returned to Dallas from the camp, someone showed up at our North Dallas home, the kind of someone you didn't see in these parts—a black pastor from South Dallas. A man my dad had just started to get to know.

The occasion? He wanted to pledge full support for the new H.I.S. BridgeBuilders organization. He offered space in his church as a temporary headquarters. My father, he said, could expect more help from him but could also expect great adversity in the days ahead.

"God greatly refines those he wants to use greatly," the man told my dad.

But he pledged to be with my father and the ministry every step of the way.

Thus was my father's "entourage" of encouragement deepening: There was my mother, Dad's constant support. Jack Graham. Mike Buster. Velma Mitchell. And now a charismatic pastor who looked at the world far differently than my father did, but who would teach much to a man who admitted, "I didn't have a clue what I was doing."

His name was E. K. Bailey.

Fifteen

THE OTHER SIDE
OF THE STORY

:::::

Dr. E. K. Bailey would walk into a room in South Dallas, and heads would turn. He was the founding pastor of Concord Missionary Baptist Church, a large, well-known church in South Dallas. He had a lot of clout nationally, as well as in the neighborhood. And he was about to link arms with a young disciple who would seem to be his polar opposite.

My father, of course.

"E. K. Bailey was bigger than life," wrote my father. His office was old-school black preacher—a big desk, big chair, the works. "African-American culture oozed from every pore of that South Dallas sanctuary, and I was a white guy from Plano," my dad wrote.

In their first meeting, months before he'd shown up on my father's doorstep, my father said he would love to work with E. K. in the inner city. Pastor Bailey asked what his plan to help the poor was. My father began to ramble on with what he called "the typical 'white man here to save you' nonsense."

Pastor Bailey listened patiently and then politely said, "I'd like to work with you, but come back another day to discuss further details." Bailey was testing my dad. He wanted to see if he was the real deal or just another do-gooder trying to absolve his guilt or build a name.

The two began meeting. E. K. was the teacher, my father the student. "Mike, if you really want to serve in this neighborhood," he said, "I want to start teaching you some of the distinctions of our culture. If you're not aware of these, they will be dividers.

"First up, articulation and voice. In our neighborhoods, you may hear what you'd consider to be yelling in your culture, but in mine I'm just talking. We're just boisterous. We speak loud, worship loud. If I'm really angry, you'll know it. So if I talk loud, don't be offended.

"Thing two: We're probably going to want to wear some clothes that are flashy and colorful, but that's what we like. Anything with bling on it. I'm going to wear something, and you're going to think it's gaudy, but not where I come from.

"Thing three: We're going to deal with things right up front and tell you exactly what's on our minds. We want to communicate who we are, and if you accept that, then good. The way we're going to change each other is to *know* each other."

Then he would ask something about my dad to do just that—get to know him better.

My father realized he had come into the area with a certain sense of pride and bravado. He needed to listen to this man.

They talked a lot about cultural nuances. For example, E. K. would refer to white people who, with a touch of self-righteousness, would say, "*I* don't see color."

"People may not mean harm when they say that, but to not see my color is to not see my pain, to not see my richness, my struggle," said Bailey. "They think it was a compliment, but God made us this way. We have something to be proud of."

Gradually, both men began modifying their views on race. My father began realizing how he naturally assumed a white perspective was the default format to which everyone should subscribe. E. K. began realizing that, as my father once wrote, "he—Bailey—leaned toward being Afrocentric, not Christocentric."

"You're not my brother, Mike," he'd tell my dad.

"Yes, I am," my dad would say. "The Bible says I am."

"There's some black men I don't even call brother," E. K. would say. "So I'm not calling you brother."

But the more time my father spent with E. K., the more impressed my father was with him. E. K., he learned, would get up every Friday morning at six o'clock to disciple 125 men. He would have the men he mentored record exactly how much time they were praying—because it reminded them of how little it actually was.

"He became my navigator," my father wrote. "He bridged the gaps. He wasn't afraid to do whatever it took to grow his community."

He helped my father see the world with new eyes. "He taught me so much about politics and the church and the ways I had judged wrongly so many things," wrote my dad. "He showed me how to love those who persecute you and attack you. He was a man of great faith and vision. One of the most brilliant preachers I have ever heard."

They laughed a lot, those two, and they disagreed—a lot. Politically, my father was more conservative than E. K. was. But even in such discussions, my father was learning. "He stretched me with some of his political views and said that the Democrats and Republicans both have biblical issues in their platforms and that I must vote more from a biblical perspective than an economic perspective. He turned my world upside down as I began to hear the other side of the story."

"E. K. and Mike didn't always see eye to eye," said Sheila Bailey, like her husband a gifted author and preacher, "but they were committed to God and to prayer. Their love for God was greater than their political differences, but it was not a cute, fuzzy relationship. Still, there was a real love between them."

E. K. told my dad that whenever he met someone new, he should ask them two questions: "How may I serve you?" and "How may I pray for you?" These are things my father took to heart; they became almost as much a part of his interaction with people as "Hello" or "How you doing?"

In addition, he constantly challenged my father, not as a means of lording it over him, but to sharpen his thinking. One day, he asked Dad why he thought so many of his African-American brothers in the ministry were not trained in conservative evangelical seminaries. Dad just figured they were liberals theologically.

"Wrong," said E. K. "It's because when they tried to enroll in your seminaries, the administrators wouldn't admit them." And if you do your homework, you'll see he's absolutely right. Decades ago, many seminaries wouldn't enroll African Americans.

And yet when BridgeBuilders had been betrayed, there was

E. K. on our doorstep to pledge his support. That meant so much to my father, coming, as it were, at one of the most vulnerable points in his life. The lesson for my father was profound: A true friend isn't just someone we hang out with or someone we agree with, politically and otherwise.

No, a true friend has our backs, no matter what.

Sixteen

GREAT EXPECTATIONS

::::

While my dad was immersing himself in the Bible and working even more among the poor of Bonton, my mother, Laura, was keeping her eye on the family financial ledger. In many ways, she was the quiet hero in all of this, the one who worked behind the scenes, who kept the books both for BridgeBuilders and the family, who balanced my father's wanderlust with a touch more practicality.

If my father was impetuous, capricious, and spontaneous, my mom had always been the quiet, steady voice of Bible-based reason. The original idea, she pointed out to my dad, was to live off the interest of the money, right? But they couldn't do that, she reminded him, if they gave away the principal too.

In September 1994, my second brother, Jonathan, was born, so Mom and Dad now had three little boys age six and under. We lived in a 2,500-square-foot house whose garage had been remodeled into an office that my folks used for BridgeBuilders. But neither of my folks had a paying job, and even if they lived in a nice house, the cupboards were getting bare.

Mom preached caution. Dad countered with his "God will

take care of us" philosophy. And continued to give their money away. By February 1996, Mom and Dad had $2,500 in their checking account and about $7,000 in investments. Amid that, my father wanted to pay someone's utility bills for $175. "Wow," my mom said, looking back on the incident. "I was not happy about that." But then the camp I was going to attend in the summer offered us a $100 scholarship. God was apparently watching out for the Fechners.

Still, if Mom sometimes worried that Dad's passion for the poor might be putting his own family at risk, she supported his new journey. As Dad deepened his spiritual roots, he couldn't help but realize that *she* was the quiet wind beneath his sometimes wildly flapping wings. And Mom couldn't help but like what she was seeing. God had truly become *God* to him, not just some genie in a bottle whose purpose was to grant him his every materialistic wish. "I could tell his encounter with Velma—and all that followed—was affecting him in a positive way," she said.

My mom had gotten to know Velma and had begun seeing in their new friend the same genuineness my father had. Meanwhile, the decision to use their million-plus dollars for the poor wasn't some hasty decision my father had made on his own.

"We both heard the prompting from God," said my mom. "We were to 'lay down our nets.' We weren't sure what it all meant at that time. But we were in this together, yes."

That said, she was fiscally cautious, and my dad could spend money with wild abandon. "He loved to shop," my mom said. And so while he wasn't spending much on himself anymore, he "shopped" a lot for the new ministry and for others who needed help.

As he continued giving away money, my dad was "counting it all joy."

"In return," he wrote, "I received a ministry education taught by God himself, and a vision for how I was to invest my life in the kingdom of God. Best of all, I finally had to depend on my heavenly Father for everything, including my daily bread."

This might sound weird, but my father didn't look at his no-money status with fear, but rather with fascination, great anticipation, and great expectation. "I was like a kid with a new pair of sneakers," he wrote. "I couldn't wait to see how fast we could run or how high we could jump." He took his renewed faith seriously and leavened it with an unforgettable laugh that suggested God was alive and bringing my father renewed joy.

Part of his boldness was learned from Velma. Early on, the two realized that if they wanted to connect with young black males—a key to changing a community like Bonton—they were going to need a gym. Not only was it one of the few places young men might want to hang out, but its versatility was appealing. The ministry could hold GED classes, afterschool programs, exercise classes, basketball—a bunch of stuff that was appealing to an array of groups.

But when my father came across a relatively new $2 million gym once run by the Dallas Housing Authority, the difference between him and Velma came to light. His faith expressed itself as a timid big toe in the swimming pool of possibilities. Velma, on the other hand, dove in headfirst without hesitation.

"We need to pray about this, Mike," she said.

He agreed. But what happened next surprised him. "I'm expecting a typical, 'O Lord, if it's your will, please give us this gym,'" he wrote. "'Would you maybe let us have it. Amen.'"

That wasn't Velma. "Lord, for your glory, we pray this gym is ours! And we tell you that we're going to use it to serve your people! And we need it, Lord, and we're just saying that we thank you for letting us have this gym, and we're believing right now that it'll be ours, Lord! I want to thank you for hearing our prayers! Amen!"

They got the gym.

That kind of spiritual brashness charged my father's batteries. His passion wasn't so much launching a new ministry; it was the wonder of how God could work through people in the process. He would work out at a gym not because he wanted to get stronger— "my mouth is my favorite muscle" he joked—but because he loved to engage people in conversation. He would chat up parents with small babies in every restaurant he ate at. Why? Because he had this unending faith that God fueled change in people if only we were willing to ignite their curiosity about him.

Then a new wrinkle entered the story. Dad's newfound enthusiasm for God—and obvious sales skills—caught the eye of Jack Graham and Mike Buster. They decided my father would be the perfect fit to lead a capital campaign to build a new $150 million campus for Plano's Prestonwood Baptist.

Right. The guy who was just beginning to immerse himself in Dallas's poorest neighborhood. A perfect fit.

Seventeen

STRADDLING THE CULTURAL LINE

::::

You could hardly have found a challenge more diametrically opposed to what my father was doing with his own money—giving it to the poor—than the Prestonwood venture. The church would be among the largest and most expensive in American history. The new structure was to be erected on a sprawling swath of Plano, 140 acres worth. The goal was to raise $32 million—and that was just for phase 1.

But here's what made my dad unique: He had a heart for people of *all* income levels. How much money you made might define you in the world's eyes, but not in God's. Wealth did not make you righteous, nor did poverty make you inferior. And neither was the reverse true. "All have sinned," my father would remind people. "Rich and poor."

He accepted the offer. True, the small stipend he'd be paid wasn't going to do much to improve our family's bottom line, but Dad believed deeper things were at work—God's kingdom and people's restoration—and he wanted to be part of those things.

I suppose he could have reasoned that Bonton was a true *need* and that a bigger, fancier church was more of a *want*. But he would argue that spiritual poverty was as much a part of Plano as it was of Bonton, that the place was filled with people who were rich in money but bankrupt in faith, as if they had sold their souls to make their millions. If it took a nice church to draw such people from darkness to light, wasn't that an investment in God's kingdom just as important as helping the poor people of Bonton?

If he said yes to Prestonwood he wasn't turning his back on BridgeBuilders and the people of Bonton. One day he would make three dozen calls to raise millions for Prestonwood; the next day he'd lead a Bible study with the poor in Bonton. The common denominator? He was all about loving and serving.

None of which paid our family's overdue electric bill, of course. If my mother had long ago seen where this was getting the family financially, it didn't hit my father until he went to the grocery store one day and realized he didn't have enough money—not even on a credit card—for food. "With effort," he said, "I tamped down a panicky feeling rising from my gut and asked the Lord for help."

Soon thereafter, he was working in South Dallas when Mom called. A Prestonwood family had heard of their financial plight and stopped by; they wanted to buy my mom and dad a freezer. "Honey," he said, "we can't eat metal. We need *food*. We don't need a freezer because we don't have the food to put in it."

"Well, babe, they still want to buy us one," my mother said.

"OK, then tell them we'll put it in the storage shed alongside the house. It's wired for power, and at least it won't be in the way out there."

The day after the freezer arrived, the woman who, along with her husband, had given it to my folks called and asked Mom if she wanted to go shopping.

"For what?"

"Well, for food, of course. We bought that freezer. It needs food in it!"

That incident was a huge "faith moment" for my father. "God listens, and he answers," my dad wrote. "And God gave me confidence in his promise to meet all our needs when we commit to seeking his kingdom and righteousness [Matthew 6:33]. That freezer full of deluxe-cut beef reminded me that [missionary] Jim Elliot was right: 'He is no fool who gives what he cannot keep to gain that which he cannot lose.'"

My father, who'd helped so many, was not against accepting help himself. Over the years, people did all sorts of things to meet our needs, and he was appreciative of the gestures, realizing that accepting help from others blessed the givers and helped complete the give/take circuit for the glory of God. And yet when someone offered us a Cadillac when we needed a car? *No thanks.* That was too much the sign of extravagance, and while my father appreciated the gesture, he politely refused it.

In the name of Christ, he also railed against something sacred in Texas—sports, particularly football. "As I see everybody so excited about football season, nowhere in the Bible do I see Jesus and the disciples talking about their alma mater and which school is theirs, who is scoring more, my team is better than yours, and all this silliness."

Dad never was philosophically opposed to sports, but he despised the *idolatry* of it. He didn't have what you might call "heroes" in his life, but the people he looked up to were not athletes. Instead of a quarterback who could thread the needle, he was more apt to admire someone like Jim Cymbala and the Brooklyn Tabernacle, with their passion to turn their neighborhood into a drug-free zone where rich and poor could worship God together.

Dad struggled with some people at Prestonwood who idolized the material things in life. How could he get them to shift their thinking? He decided the answer was this: *being the change he wanted to see in others.* Letting his life, his choices, his values be the lesson.

He didn't intentionally give away his million-plus dollars to impress anyone. He did it because he believed it was what God wanted of him. At any rate, a man helping raise tens of millions of dollars for a church in upscale Plano, Texas, was now, in essence, broke himself.

The million-plus dollars he had only three years ago? Gone. Every cent of it.

Eighteen

WALKING THE TALK

::::

Some people may have seen my father as a leaf on a river, going wherever the currents took him. I believe he saw himself as a vessel of God, plying uncharted waters with the zeal of a pirate. He was a modern-day Noah, not necessarily understanding what lay ahead but more than willing to roll up his sleeves and start building a boat, even if people might be laughing at him.

His old values system had been blown up. It was replaced with one that—short of his Achilles' heel forays into Nordstrom—might have fit more appropriately into the Jesus movement of the 1960s and '70s. He no longer was dragging God along on his self-indulgent journey to material bliss, but he was listening to where God wanted him to go, a sort of spiritual hippie in well-buffed penny loafers, a cuffed button-down, and a ring with a cross on it.

"In the years that followed, I rested in God's confidence," he said. "Better yet, I *soared* in his confidence."

By the late 1990s—about a decade since the focus of his life had begun to shift—my father was leading one of the largest capital campaigns in U.S. church history. For the first phase of the project, Prestonwood's goal was to raise $32 million. Despite being essentially broke himself, my dad helped raise $36 million.

Although he received a small stipend from the church for heading the fund-raising, we were eating donated meat from a donated freezer and barely making our monthly financial obligations. Then out of the blue, in 1997, Jack Graham offered my father a full-time position as a minister at the church. This was not a "let's save the Fechners" life ring, but a means to further the kingdom of God by involving a proven teacher and a natural leader.

My mother was relieved; this would mean an actual paycheck. Insurance. Security. My father was relieved for her—and anxious to see how God was going to help him juggle a couple of weighty tasks. Never mind that he now had a full-time job. Never mind that my parents now had a daughter, Grace (born in 1996), which gave my thirty-six-year-old mom and thirty-five-year-old dad four children under the age of eight. Dad not only didn't give up BridgeBuilders, but the ministry experienced huge expansion in the late 1990s and early 2000s.

At Prestonwood, the young marrieds classes Dad was teaching were thriving, not just in numbers, but in changed lives. Meanwhile, BridgeBuilders was morphing into much more than it once was.

In 1999—the same year Prestonwood opened its new church—my dad encouraged our family optometrist, Dr. Kim Castleberry, to take a tour of BridgeBuilders. The man was smitten with the ministry from the get-go. Soon, he started a Patch Adams operation in a space the Dallas Housing Authority allowed the ministry to use. In time, Dr. Castleberry would build a partnership between BridgeBuilders and the University of Houston College of Optometry to expand into a full-service optical clinic. In addition, in 2003, the ministry started a lens lab and dispensary.

Velma worked with seminarians from Dallas Theological Seminary and Southwestern Baptist Theological Seminary to do Bible studies in Bonton.

In 2004, my dad's parents launched BridgeBuilders' first satellite ministry in San Antonio. Dad's twin brother, Mel, became the new ministry's manager about a year later. More branches would come. For now, my dad concentrated on raising money, leading Bible studies, and building more bridges to folks in Bonton—all on top of his job at Prestonwood.

While some ministers take Fridays off, Dad used that day of the week to focus 100 percent on BridgeBuilders. Then, despite being part of Prestonwood's Saturday night service, he would go to Bonton on Saturday morning.

He worked nonstop. Some might think, *When did this guy have time to play golf or tailgate before a football game?* He didn't, plain and simple. With rare exceptions, he did nothing that others might consider "fun." But here's the deal: He considered ministry itself fun. Honest. He didn't see it as drudgery, as trying to score points with God, or as a way to alleviate any guilt he might have had. No, he loved people. He loved God. So why wouldn't he want to spend most of his life involved with building the King's kingdom? I never once heard my father lament that he'd rather be doing this or that. He loved serving, plain and simple.

Still, some wondered about his family. Were we neglected? Absolutely not. From the moment he hit the door, it was family time. Dad didn't take any "me time" to be alone. He also took us with him whenever possible to do ministry, whether in Bonton or at Prestonwood. Dad and I had some great conversations during the one-hour round-trip drive to Bonton from our home in Plano. He gave every minute to us or to someone in need.

Meanwhile, as word about the bridge to Bonton spread, more Prestonwood people were getting involved in the ministry, even if at times the cultural wall between the two cultures was high. One Prestonwood member, Jeri, was helping a Bonton teenager with her reading so she could earn her GED. But progress was slow.

"I was pretty sure that either I had misheard God's call or God had mis-called," she said. "The young woman, Tia, struggled, I struggled. She often came to school sick. One day, when she was pretty ill, I suggested we just sit and talk instead of doing academic work. Slowly she began to share with me about her family, and I told her about mine. She told me she had been to prison for aggravated assault. We both laughed when she added, 'But I'm not aggravated no mo, Miss Jeri.'"

The incident sparked the beginning of a true and precious relationship between the two. The lesson? "If we'll take the time and effort to get to know each other," my father said, "we'll be reminded we are two human beings created by God for his glory." And, as such, more likely to seek the best in one another.

Nineteen

BROTHER TO BROTHER

::::

What mattered to my father was as much about processes as about results. Sure, he wanted to ultimately "win" something for BridgeBuilders a gym, a Habitat for Humanity home, an eye specialist willing to serve a couple of days a week. But he loved the "getting there" just as much, maybe more. Loved what he could learn from those who partnered with him. Loved to see the myriad ways God could make the impossible possible through the people He brought into Dad's life.

And E. K. Bailey knew the kind of people my dad needed to know.

If my father was sold on E. K. from the get-go, it took some time for E. K. to ascertain that Dad was the real deal. And who could blame his caution? Over the years, in South Dallas, E. K. had watched white politician after white politician storm into the ghetto during campaign season, promise help for the poor, smile for some ribbon-cutting ceremony, and never be heard from again.

"I confess that I've been skeptical of whites who came to me, reaching out, because we all have been bitten and deceived, and

we have asked, 'OK, what's your game? What are you pushing?'" E. K. once said in a dialogue with Warren Wiersbe about
preaching.*

But E. K. began to realize my dad was different. "I noticed
that Mike was genuine," he said to Wiersbe. "In the African-
American community, to call someone of another race 'genuine'
is to say a lot. First, it says that he does not come with the typical
white agenda that we see being practiced so often . . . Second,
Mike did not come with a prescribed idea about what we needed
in our community. Third, he did not come with the attitude that
here is a white man who has solutions to all of the problems in
the African-American community. In terms of attitude, he simply
came as a humble brother who genuinely loved God and people.
He prayed for God to guide him to the right people that he could
partner with, who also had the same goals and desires to help this
disenfranchised and disinherited African-American community."†

In decades as a pastor, E. K. could easily discern "talk" from
"walk." He held people to high standards. But my father, he
soon realized, proved himself not only with his words but with
his actions as well.

E. K. tried to find some sort of hidden motive in my father,
but couldn't. "I could tell Mike was genuine when he walked
into the homes of the people in the projects and sat down and ate
their food," E. K. Bailey told Wiersbe. "I knew he was genuine
when he hugged little snotty-nosed black children. He cared for

---

* E. K. Bailey and Warren W. Wiersbe, *Preaching in Black and White: What We
Can Learn from Each Other* (Grand Rapids: Zondervan, 2003), 131.
† Ibid., 131–32.

them as though they were his own. I knew he was genuine when he took his own family to fellowship, socialize, and have fun with children who were undereducated and exposed to drugs and every unimaginable thing you could experience in society. I knew he was genuine when he asked the men of our church and the men of his church, at that time in far North Dallas, to come way down to the projects in South Dallas to meet and have fellowship over breakfast."*

"It was important to Dad that we be there, so it was important to us," said my brother Jonathan, who remembers the trips even when he was small. "It was almost just like a big family gathering every Saturday. On paper, it doesn't sound that appealing, but it was fun. And over time you'd see that it was actually changing people's lives."

Once, E. K. took my father to one of his favorite restaurants in South Dallas. E. K. was wearing an African-themed short-sleeved shirt with a hat, and my father was wearing a suit. When it came time to pay the bill, the server, who was African American, placed the bill by my dad, not by E. K., as if my father certainly was the one taking the other man to lunch.

"Mike," E. K. said, "give me the bill. I know you don't have any money. I'll let you pay with my $100 bill so the waiter will think you bought the poor black man a meal." Then he laughed heartily.

My dad and mom joined a group that E. K. and his wife, Sheila, had started, an in-home series of forums meant to bring

---

* Ibid., 132.

down racial barriers. People of different ethnic backgrounds would watch a movie or read a book—say, *To Kill a Mockingbird*—and then discuss it from a racial perspective.

Dad asked E. K. to serve on the H.I.S. BridgeBuilders board. E. K. asked Dad to serve on the board of E. K. Bailey Ministries, Inc. Dad asked E. K. to speak at Prestonwood Baptist and arranged for him to speak to three thousand singles as part of a citywide organization. E. K. asked Dad to preach at his church, something Pastor Bailey rarely allowed anyone but himself to do.

The key to their friendship was the understanding that you don't love someone because they see the world exactly as you do, vote for the same politicians you do, or value everything you do. You love someone because you care about them as another human being and look for the best in them.

"We differed strongly on some political issues and on issues that he was involved with in his church," said E. K. in his conversation with Warren Wiersbe. "Now, that was the test that will either make or break it. Again he took the initiative as he said, 'E. K., you're my brother, and I'm not going to allow this to separate me from you.' We can't say, 'You can be my friend until we disagree over critical issues. Then we separate along racial or political lines.' It did not happen. We fought our way through and remained committed to each other."*

E. K. was forever putting on large conferences for preachers. Often, my dad would be the only white person in the room, except for the times he took me with him. To say it was a

---

* Ibid., 134.

cultural shock for a kid who grew up going to the conservative Prestonwood Church would be an understatement. But, like my dad, I grew to love these conferences and occasionally attended Concord to hear Pastor Bailey preach.

Once, my father was invited to a huge ministry conference whose theme was understanding the nuances of black and white cultures. My father was sitting in the back when a member of E. K.'s "entourage" came to him.

"Mike," he said, "E. K. and Sheila would like you to sit at the head table with them."

Dad had a sort of "Who, me?" look on his face.

"This is my brother," E. K. later told the audience. "Take care of him."

In years to come, my father's relationship with E. K. opened doors right and left. My dad would be somewhere, and someone would come up to him and say, "Are you *the one*? Are you E. K.'s brother?"

"Yes," my dad would say.

"Fine," would come the reply. "How can we help you? How can we pray for you?"

Twenty

MAKING DISCIPLES

:::::

Dad's relationship with E. K. Bailey opened some important doors for him, no doubt about it. But on the street, what bought him credibility was how he related so well to the everyday folks who didn't have the prestige of an E. K. Bailey.

Twenty miles north, in Plano, my father built the same credibility with folks who drove new cars, wore three-piece suits, and worked in plush office buildings—guys my father would be discipling.

"Mike Fechner walked the talk," said Jarrett Stephens, who was my dad's first intern at Prestonwood. And the talk was this: Rich or poor, black or white, Plano or Bonton, we are all sinners saved by the loving grace of God.

"That was his microcosm of utopia: a mixture of black and white, rich and poor. He was truly a bridge builder," said Stephens. "He could bring North Dallas and South Dallas together. He could talk white, and he could talk black."

As Dad transitioned from being mentored to mentoring and discipling young black men in Bonton, he was taking the interns at Prestonwood under his wings too. He set the bar high for his "boys." The Bible was to be read daily, in depth. Prayer wasn't to be uttered with the anxiousness of a "one-Mississippi, two-Mississippi . . ." pass-rusher count in street football, but pursued slowly, diligently, reverently. And each young man's walk was as important, or more important, than his talk.

"Mike Fechner was the most influential guy in my life," said Stephens, who, socioeconomically, couldn't have been more different from those young men in Bonton. But, like them, he saw Mike as a father figure. Beyond that, Stephens saw someone who made those around him better. "Few people go out every day to help sharpen others," he said. "That's what Mike was—a sharpener."

"Everybody Mike touched was more kingdom minded," said Mary Anderwald, who would soon become Dad's administrative assistant. "The young men in the community of Bonton called him 'Dad.' He was a spiritual father to a lot of men who had never had a real dad."

He challenged. He taught. He prayed. He listened. He guided. All with a sense that what mattered wasn't where you lived or what your past had been like, but where your heart was. Some people, he'd say, got hung up on being conservatives or liberals, Republicans or Democrats. My father thought, as Christians, we needed to transcend such labels.

"He'd point out that, historically, evangelicals were all about preaching the gospel but didn't do much to clothe the naked, feed the hungry, or take care of the sick," said Stephens. "And liberals take care of everything but don't share the gospel. Mike couldn't work in either of those contexts alone. He was involved in both."

My dad was spiritually astute enough to realize that, deep down, the young men at Prestonwood and the young men in Bonton had the same needs. On the surface, of course, you wouldn't think the two had anything in common.

The well-to-do men in North Dallas, usually white, sometimes struggled—as my father had earlier in his life—to get real with themselves. It's hard to be humble when you're tooling down the street in a BMW and have your own gardener. But that doesn't mean you're not aching inside for what really matters.

At the same time, drug dealers and pimps in Bonton sometimes struggled—as my father had—to get real with themselves. It's hard to be humble when you're tooling down the street in a low-rider and your only currency is your street cred of being a tough, bad man. But, like the young men in North Dallas, that doesn't mean you're not aching inside for what really matters.

By now I was in my teens, and Dad would increasingly involve me in experiences he knew would widen my perspective or deepen my faith. Meanwhile, he would increasingly teach me—through his actions—that God's grace wasn't just something to appreciate, but something to give to others.

Once, our family was going to our favorite Mexican restaurant, a place called El Fenix in downtown Dallas, which was a convenient stop on the way back from Bonton. "As we walked toward the restaurant, we blew right past this homeless guy on the street who was begging for spare change," remembers my brother Jonathan. "We were all hungry and being selfish. But Dad stopped and asked, 'What do you need? Do you need money?' The guy nodded his head yes. So Dad handed him a $20 bill. But Dad didn't just walk away feeling smug, like he'd done his job. He talked to the guy for a few minutes. After about five minutes, Dad waved us all over to join him. And right there in the parking lot, we all prayed over this guy."

The young man started crying. "I just lied to you," he said. "I feel terrible. I'm not homeless. I'm a student trying to make some extra money." He handed my father back the $20 bill.

"My dad," recalled Jonathan, "took it, put it back in his hand, and said, 'Christ provides forgiveness.'"

That was my dad. Every moment was a teachable moment. Some such lessons involved simple words or gestures, like the one in front of the Mexican restaurant. Others were, shall we say, a bit more complex and risky.

Twenty-One

DARING TO
ENLIGHTEN

:::::

In 2001, when my dad brought Sharon Emmert from Preston-wood into the BridgeBuilders ministry, Velma wasn't doing handstands. Sharon was a former flight attendant—petite, powerful, and perky, a take-charge person who was a bit too much for Velma, who was none of those things.

"They were," said my father, "like oil and water." Sharon was corporate America; Velma was backwoods Texas—at least in the eyes of Velma. Sharon was way too "together" all the time; Velma struggled.

In a similar situation, some managers might have moved one of the women to a new position so she wouldn't have to work with the other. Instead, my father prayed and then sent the pair to Minnesota to attend a conference, where they would share a hotel room. Velma was aghast. It was hard enough just working with this woman, but to be *roommates*?

They came back, as Velma said, "joined at the hip, as if she was my bud," which tickled my father to death. He loved to show people how God can do what we can't—in this case, heal a broken relationship.

On the plane trip home, Velma melted into tears. "I'm like, God, you are such an awesome God to give me the opportunity to know such an awesome person. And to know what true Christian love is all about. It's not about those things I was taught growing up—white people this, white people that."

As my father deepened his commitment to Prestonwood and to BridgeBuilders, he was forever looking for ways to bridge the two cultures. Once, he hit on what he knew was a high-risk, high-reward idea. But my father was nothing if not a risk taker.

At times, he would be asked to speak at youth camps. When charged with accompanying five dozen kids by bus to camp in Colorado, he got an idea for a teachable moment (not quite like giving away his $1-million-plus money—he'd already done that—but it wasn't small potatoes in the risk category either): Have Velma pose as a homeless woman at a truck stop. When the bus made a stop there, hope someone invites her along to the camp as a way to teach kids to interact with someone far different from them.

Velma was all in. Beyond dressing in rags, she was so intent on being convincing that she blacked out a couple of her teeth. She flew to Wichita Falls, Texas, for the well-planned scheme. But the reaction from the kids at the truck stop horrified my father.

At first, Velma asked for a little money for a sandwich. None of the kids paid her any attention. The adult chaperones, much to Dad's dismay, were more standoffish than the kids, one of whom finally offered her a biscuit.

Finally a young girl and her friends began talking to Velma and seeing how they could help. One ultimately came to Dad. "I know you are the camp pastor, and I have to share something with you," she said. "I had a dream we would be entertaining angels unaware on this trip. That homeless lady is of God, and she may be an angel. We have to take her with us."

My father was quietly overjoyed. This was exactly what he'd hoped for in the first place. At the girl's urging, he invited Velma to come along on the bus to Colorado. The ride was ten hours long. Only the one girl paid Velma any attention, though she did so intensely, talking to her, listening to her, and giving her a new Bible.

Once at the camp in Colorado, my dad spoke to the group of kids on how the disciples had ignored the woman at the well but Jesus had engaged her in conversation—despite the woman being at the bottom of the societal chain and in the "wrong" ethnic group. He shared how sinful it is to judge others because of race, education, or any other worldly standard. He definitely had their attention. The room quieted to a hush.

"And now," he said, "I'd like you to meet my sister."

Out walked Velma. Jaws dropped. Velma, now being totally herself and not the homeless character she portrayed, began sharing how it felt to have been snubbed by so many—and how good it felt to have been accepted by the one student. Tears among the teenagers flowed freely.

"That night," my father later wrote, "the Spirit of God convicted dozens of students to repent of their self-righteousness and surrender to the lordship of Christ."

Thirty prayed to receive Christ as their Savior. For the rest of the week, you would have thought Velma was a rock star. All the kids wanted her to stay in their cabin and pray with them and share her stories of God's goodness.

Sadly, the adult chaperones weren't as pliable—or repentant—as their children. "It was ironic that even after God showed up and the youth began to be rekindled with their need for repentance and returning to Jesus, many of the adults seemed entrenched in their distance from me and Velma," he wrote. "I never knew why, except for the possible pain of the conviction of the Holy Spirit on their own hearts and souls."

But it's not as if Dad would dwell on such shortcomings—any more than he would dwell on his own. He looked for the good in people, choosing to honor the way the kids on the trip overcame their biases, rather than to bad-mouth the adults who did not. At every turn in life, he took advantage of opportunities to teach and learn. The world was his oyster, and, while exploring it, he wasn't going to miss opportunities. Nor was he going to waste time.

After all, you never knew how much of it you had left.

Twenty-Two

THE FIRST GOOD-BYE

:::::

In 2001, the news rippled through the African-American community in South Dallas like an earthquake: At age fifty-five, my father's decade-long friend and mentor, E. K. Bailey, had been diagnosed with lung cancer.

My dad marveled as, amid the news, his friend calmly faced the future. E. K. encouraged his board at Concord to have Bryan Carter, a young man he had mentored for years, be his replacement when he died. He prayed. And he kept teaching my father.

As their weekly get-togethers continued, E. K. began spending more and more time talking about cancer. Not so much about the general idea that he had it, but about dealing with it medically. "Now, Mike, when you get cancer, they try to put you in a rut and push you down, just try to give you one kind of medicine," E. K. would say, "but I tell you, there's great stuff in the homeopathic world, and I'm going to Mexico to do some stuff there. Don't be limited. Let the Lord lead you."

E. K. would go on for hours about his illness, almost as if my father had asked for advice, though he hadn't. And my dad would think, *Why is he teaching me this? Why all this detail* about cancer?

Christmas was coming. My father's gusto for holiday decorating was akin to Texas's gusto for football. He would orchestrate the decorating of our house like a conductor leads an orchestra—and had noted how, when E. K. came to our house during the holidays, he loved the way my father decorated.

And so as Christmas 2002 neared, E. K. was on Dad's mind. "I don't think for sure he knew it would be his last," wrote my father, "but the Lord laid it on my heart: *Go to E. K.'s house and put up some wreaths.*"

Ha! "Some wreaths" turned into a full-blown adorning of the Bailey home in lavish but tasteful Christmas decor, a virtual winter wonderland complete with a "fruit of the Spirit" theme. Dad brought his family and a few interns with him; by then, at fourteen, I was the oldest and Grace, six, the youngest of the four kids. Garland here, poinsettia there. Bells and mistletoe. We arrived at six o'clock and didn't leave until nearly midnight, enjoying a feast of fried chicken in between.

"Sheila said to do it any way you want to," my father wrote. "It was such a simple thing, but such an honor. And I loved to celebrate Christ's birthday this way. Here, I got to do it for my brother. He just laughed. He was just full of joy."

E. K. died the next autumn.

Shortly before E. K. passed, my father went to see him at Methodist Dallas Medical Center, having been notified that Pastor Bailey didn't have much time left. "It was so surreal," Dad remembered. "He was a true giant of the faith. He battled cancer so optimistically, so joyfully, investing in others, investing in me, loving life. He still looked good. Weaker, but still full, not like he was close to death. And so I prayed—some of the elders were there—and said good-bye and started to cry."

"Don't you cry, brother," E. K. told my dad. "There's no crying, only celebration. This is a good thing."

He said it in a firm, low voice, almost a whisper. Dad loved E. K.—"he was my advocate, my watch guard, my elder"—and didn't want to disappoint him in any way. So he stopped crying. Then, in the elevator as he left the hospital, the dam burst. He wept all the way home.

My father spoke at one of three services that were held to remember E. K., then went into contemplative questioning about why God allowed a man of such stature to die at the relatively young age of fifty-seven, a nonsmoker succumbing to lung cancer. "Why death?" he wrote. "We prayed for E. K.'s healing. He's a man of God. Why didn't God answer this prayer 'yes'?"

This is the answer my dad settled on: "E. K. and Sheila are two of the greatest people of faith I've ever known. When he died, it was his appointed time to die. She was then able to do more for the kingdom."

He likened it to Moses leading his people out of the wilderness and then dying, and God turning the reins over to Joshua. "That's what E. K. did with Bryan Carter. He established the church, cast the vision, got it running, and then he handed it over. Pastor Carter has possessed the promised land."

We live our lives in seasons whose comings and goings are orchestrated by God, reasoned my father. "E. K.'s time was appointed. He had fulfilled his role in bringing glory to God. The seed has a season. One plants, one waters, one reaps." E. K.

had planted. Someone else, perhaps Carter, would be the one who reaps.

Dad referred to a time when E. K. was sick and Sheila was invited to go to London and speak with Anne Graham Lotz, Billy Graham's daughter. Everybody, including E. K., was telling her she should go. But Sheila wasn't so sure. She called my dad for advice.

"What do you think you should do?" he asked.

"No, I want to know what *you* think I should do," she responded.

My dad paused a moment. "Your husband needs you right now," he said. "You're never going to get these days back."

She paused. "I knew you'd say that. I knew you would tell me the truth." She started to cry.

"If you do what's right in God's eyes," he said, "he'll give you the opportunities and more."

She agreed. She didn't go.

In the months after E. K. died, my father went back to Concord numerous times. Among other things, he encouraged Sheila Bailey in her decision to launch a national ministry focused on women.

Once, he poked his head in the room where he and E. K. would eat lunch and talk on and on about their respective cultures and how Jesus was the bridge between them. E. K.'s photo was on the wall. My father looked at it and thought of the man behind the smile.

"BridgeBuilders would not be where it is today without E. K. Bailey," he later wrote.

The seasons of life, he was reminded, aren't ours to choose. *One plants, one waters, one reaps.* But first one *trusts.* Sheila Bailey would, again, be asked to go to London and would say yes this time. And my father would find himself becoming more and more like his friend E. K. Bailey.

Twenty-Three

CULTURALLY
AMBIDEXTROUS

::::

My father never forgot the story about his mother being scolded for trying to buy the maid a Coke at a drugstore in Fort Worth. Nor did he forget the incident in Virginia when his black friends were the targets of racial slurs. And he never forgot the experience of being on the other end of racism when, as a white kid, he was a minority student in Hawaii.

But when it came to Velma and E. K. Bailey and other African Americans, his respect for—and defense of—them was never solely *because* they were black. It was because they were people, period. Because of their spirits, determination, and uniqueness. He never forgot E. K. Bailey's insistence that others *not* ignore their color—that they *not* pretend color didn't exist or puff themselves up with the unrealistic idea that "we are all the same." The fact is, we weren't all the same, though we all should be treated with respect.

Still, you couldn't help but notice every time we'd go to a restaurant, if there was a family with a black baby, that little kid was probably going to wind up being kitchy-kitchy-kooed by my dad, if not rocked in his arms. Suffice it to say that African Americans—even those he didn't know and would never meet—found a special place in his heart.

"When he looked in the mirror, I think he saw a black man," said Jarrett Stephens, with tongue only slightly in cheek. "It wasn't a put-on, but because he immersed himself so deeply into the lives of that community and knew firsthand of their struggles and believed in them. That was just him."

If my father had a rebel streak in him—and, like me, he did—it wasn't about drawing attention to himself or about being ornery or contrarian. It was that he thought, as Christians, we had a biblical mandate to love people where they were and help them follow Jesus. Period. The world wasn't made up of good guys and bad guys. No, the line of evil ran through every human heart.

My dad was amazed by the disdain that North Dallas people had for South Dallas sin and that South Dallas people had for North Dallas sin. It was normally the folks from North Dallas who were more condemning of their counterparts to the south.

Take, for instance, smoking cigarettes. Many in the community and church I grew up in would say, "How can you do that? Your body is the temple of God." And yet when it comes to materialism and gluttony, we have a plank bigger than Noah's ark in our own eyes. The point, my father would say, is not to rag on one group or the other, but to realize that just because our sins are different or yours may be more visible, I am no better than you are. So instead of condemning, let's encourage and learn from one another, not cutting down but sharpening each other.

"I never saw anyone who could engage a homeless guy on the street just as easily as he could a millionaire," said Mike Buster.

When Dad first hired Jarrett Stephens at Prestonwood, the first thing he said was, "We need to get you some clothes." He knew Jarrett had only three hundred dollars to his name, so he took him down to Men's Warehouse and bought him a new suit. "Mike is the most giving man I've ever met," said Stephens.

The second thing he did was take Jarrett to Bonton and have him lead devotions before games in the basketball league. "All these African Americans and me, the white boy," he recalled with a laugh.

It was as if Dad was culturally ambidextrous. He might pray with a Bonton drug dealer in the morning and challenge a Highland Park millionaire to walk his Christian talk in the afternoon.

Once, a close friend of my dad's, Matthew McIntyre, was driving to a fund-raiser that my father was doing for BridgeBuilders. Matthew runs a life insurance company that has offices in sixteen states, has fifty thousand clients, and did $125 million in sales in 2013.

"Don't you be spending anything on anybody," the firm's corporate chaplain—yes, in Texas, some companies have chaplains—told him en route to the event. The company's charitable coffers were all but dry, he reminded McIntyre.

The chaplain dropped him off, ran some errands, and returned to pick him up when the lunch was over.

"Tell me you didn't pledge anything," said the chaplain. Matthew didn't say a word but just sat there with a wide grin.

"Tell me you didn't go crazy and give, like, ten thousand dollars," said the chaplain.

The grin widened. "I didn't go crazy and give ten thousand dollars," said Matthew.

About the time the chaplain was sighing with relief, Matthew said, "I gave five hundred thousand dollars."

True story. Matthew was taken by my father's courage. "He gets up in front of all these influential businessmen and tells it like it is," he said. "I'm thinking, 'This guy is gutsy.' He actually believes what the Bible says and knows what can be done with that money and there is no plan B. It's like, 'Here's the Jordan, and I'm crossing it.' I thought, *All right*, and wrote out that pledge. But here's the thing: he didn't treat you any differently depending on how much you gave. He didn't care if you gave a dime or five hundred thousand dollars. I've never seen anything like it."

Twenty-Four

LEAD, FOLLOW, OR
GET OUT OF THE WAY

::::

"Nobody could talk money out of people like Mike Fechner," said
Jarrett Stephens. "Nobody."

But only if the giver truly believed in the cause, which was
usually the case. An amazingly high percentage of BridgeBuilders'
biggest donors came to Bonton and helped out, tutoring or mentoring or pulling weeds or painting fences. Sometimes, however,
Dad would run into people who were giving money with a
sort of Pharisee-like attitude. Like, *Aren't I something, doing you
this favor?*

"He would tell them to keep it," said McIntyre. "If their heart
wasn't in it, forget it. Likewise, someone would give a quarter of
a million dollars and demand a seat on the board or some other
influence. He wouldn't play that game. Oh, and he also hated it
when people of means gave some tawdry gift and acted as if they
were special, like right before Christmas donating old stuff they
wouldn't give to their own dog."

Whether it was for a 7,500-seat sanctuary in Plano that was

going to draw wealthy people to hear the gospel, or fifteen thousand dollars to feed Bonton families turkey on Christmas, there would always be provision. Dad would ask in faith and watch God come through over and over again.

If he sometimes saw himself as the general of his own brigade, his unspoken orders were, "Lead, follow, or get out of the way." That go-go-go attitude could, at times, ruffle feathers. He wanted everyone to be running as fast as he was, to be as passionate as he was. Not that he was a steamroller who ignored everyone around him.

"Mike taught me about grace because he was so quick to *give* grace," said Mary Anderwald, my dad's assistant. "There were times over the years when something I did or failed to do caused problems for the ministry. He was always quick to forgive and to instruct on how to untangle the results and prevent future problems."

But, without a doubt, he had high standards. After I hadn't received any sort of football award in eighth grade—and roughly half the team *did*—I was whining about it. Dad looked me in the eye. "Michael, if you want something, you have to work your butt off for it, and you didn't—so quit crying and complaining." He was quick to build me back up, though. "Do you want to be great at football? If so, I'll help you get there." And he did.

Just like he was there to help me—an insecure kid who mumbled in front of other people—break out of my shell and feel comfortable speaking in front of crowds. Was it sometimes painful, his sitting down with me and encouraging me to enunciate my words clearly? Absolutely. I hated it. "Just leave me alone," I wanted to say. Or, "Can't you just accept me as I am?" But was it worth it? Yes.

"I have never been so lovingly rebuked by anyone as that guy," said Matthew McIntyre. "I mean, here I am, a CEO of a company, and he used to tell me something I needed to improve on, then show me something, and I never felt hammered on. He had a unique ability to do that."

Dad's imagination was endless, and his passion boundless, but he never would have accomplished what he did without the support of Mom. She was this quiet force that kept him going, this rock of stability while he was bouncing from here to there.

Countless men came to our house to meet with Dad about marital issues because of the ministry. Typically, it had something to do with the guy's wife not wanting to change their lifestyle just because her husband had come to Jesus. Many men felt threatened by their wives, who might decide to leave them because "this isn't what I signed up for." I saw it happen time and again. Despite the example in John 12:42–43 about Pharisees who loved praise from other people more than from God, the guy would turn his back on the call of Christ in his life for fear of retribution

Mom was strong and solid. The main thing I wanted in a wife was someone who was always going to be open to wherever the Lord leads—a servant of the Lord, not a slave to the world.

Never mind that Dad could inspire a donation of half a million dollars with a single speech; when money for the ministry ran low in 2004, he chose to put our family's house on the sales block. The vision of doing grand things with a ministry for

God's glory wasn't going to let a few hundred thousand dollars get in the way. And if that meant selling the dream house, then so be it.

In Mark 10:21, hadn't Jesus told the rich young ruler, "Go, sell everything you have and give to the poor, and you will have treasure in heaven. Then come, follow me"? My father had already done it once in the early 1990s when he sold his business and surrendered to ministry, and that's exactly what he was doing again.

Three days after the house was listed, the phone rang.

"Mike, you don't know me," a man told my father, "but I know about you, and I saw in the newspaper that your house was for sale. God prompted me to call you. Is there something wrong with the house?"

"Nothing at all wrong with the house," said my dad. "Great condition. Big backyard. Five bedrooms. Downstairs office."

"Mike, I'm not interested in buying the house," the man said. "Why are you selling it?"

My father didn't hesitate. "We need funding for our ministry," he said. A slight pause ensued.

"Mike," the stranger said, "I'll cover whatever need your ministry has."

The stranger-turned-friend, a man named Thomas, made good on that promise in the next few days. My parents kept the house. And the ministry continued to flourish, even if at times we weren't as enthusiastic as Dad.

My brothers and I grew up loving football. On Saturdays,

when my dream was starting off with College GameDay followed by twelve uninterrupted hours of football watching, chips and queso stuffing, and soda guzzling, Dad would suddenly appear.

"Who wants to go to Bonton with me?" he'd ask.

Dad knew we didn't want to, but he also knew I knew that going to Bonton is what Christ would be doing instead of wasting the day on football. Sometimes I stood strong; "Nope," I'd say, "I'm going to stay home." But after two hours of watching football, I couldn't help but think what a stupid decision I'd made—choosing football over ministering to and loving the people of Bonton.

Dad hardly ever watched TV. He had no hobbies. And about the only sports events he attended were the ones his children were involved in. During one of my football games at Prestonwood Christian Academy, he started a "We believe!" cheer that soon had our entire fan base joining in. It became the unofficial motto of the football program and remains that way more than ten years after he started it. That was my dad—daring to do something different and inspiring others to follow him for a cause beyond himself.

The young men who worked under him at Prestonwood— by then, Dad was in his early forties—quickly became like family, like older brothers to my siblings and me. In fact, one of the interns, Joshua Rolf, actually moved in with our family for a couple of years.

"I'd sleep up in the game room, and Laura would take the kids to school; and I'd look over the balcony, and there would be

Mike, sprawled out on a big pillow, praying, journaling, reading his Bible," Joshua said. "He'd pray over nearly every name in the church."

"He was this larger-than-life guy," said Joshua. "He wanted to do something great for the kingdom of God."

And he did. In fact, the fruits of his labor were just starting to show.

Twenty-Five

THE FIRST TO
STEP FORWARD

::::

Soon after I graduated from high school in 2006 and started a summer internship with H.I.S. BridgeBuilders, you could measure the success of the ministry in a few ways. You could look at the eye clinic, the new dental clinic, the Adopt-a-Block program, or Operation Cleanup. You could look at all sorts of physical changes in Bonton. Old, worthless drug dens bulldozed and replaced by new Habitat for Humanity homes. The closing of the Turner Courts and Rhoads Terrace housing developments—broken-down buildings rife with drug deals and prostitution—and the building of new apartments. You could interview guys like Chris Tedford, a friend of my father's who started a job-training program for Bonton men at his machine shop. You could talk to the police, who weren't having to intervene as much as they once had.

Or you could look at something else. The changed lives of people in Bonton—in particular, the lives of young men such as Rodrick Yarbrough.

To understand Rodrick, let me take you back to a moment when he was twenty-seven years old. He was well established, making good money, highly respected among his peers. Come to think of it, he was much like my father was at the same age. Only he wasn't making his big money by selling home security systems to Plano newcomers chasing the American Dream; he was making it by selling drugs, primarily grass, to Bonton bad boys who made this neighborhood a nightmare.

He had come in one night to his ramshackle apartment and was quietly celebrating his success by rolling a joint, a process no less a part of his daily routine as getting dressed.

"Daddy, what are you doing?"

It was his three-year-old son, Rodrick Jr. He pushed his son aside and ran downstairs to get something he'd forgotten. When he returned, he saw it—the little boy rolling a piece of paper as if preparing a joint of his own.

In that moment, it was as if all the rationalization, all the denial, all the "I don't need any help" bravado melted like a block of ice in front of a blowtorch. Rodrick couldn't run anymore. It was too real, too convicting, too powerful—this thought of his son becoming who he was.

Just as their fathers were, many of the young men in Bonton are disengaged from their families. But those who are engaged with their kids too often believe that by selling drugs, stealing, or pimping they are providing a way out for their children because they'll have money to provide things for them. And kids naturally follow the example their fathers set for them.

So Rodrick's noticing this—and being bothered by it—

marked the first step in his becoming a new man, just as my father had. The gospel of Luke speaks of the prodigal son changing "when he came to his senses" (Luke 15:17). That night, Rodrick came to his senses. That's how people change. That's how neighborhoods change.

My father had come to realize something about turning around places steeped in poverty: If Bonton was going to change, it would only happen with buy-in from at least some of the young males whom other young men respected.

That's not a slam on women; in fact, it's more of a slam on men. They are the ones who so often make selfish choices that damage the neighborhood—doing drugs, selling drugs, getting young women pregnant but not supporting the mother or child, exploiting women through prostitution, and more. In years hence, President Obama would essentially suggest the same thing with his Fatherhood Initiative aimed at young men taking responsibility for the benefit of others.

At any rate, my father realized that Rodrick was one Bonton leader he needed to reach. And reach him he did. At a Monday night pickup basketball game in the same gym for which Velma had prayed with gusto, Rodrick made a commitment to Christ, in part because of the encouragement of one of the counselors who'd come down from North Dallas that evening—my father.

By this point in Dad's life, the early 2000s, he had gotten to be a fairly big deal in evangelical circles. He was speaking at conferences. He had raised $36 million for Prestonwood Baptist Church. And he had been invited to Washington, D.C., to offer a prayer as part of the National Day of Prayer. He and my mother would be sitting with the Joint Chiefs of Staff, Senator Hillary Clinton, and the president's cabinet. Front row, three seats down from the president of the United States, George W. Bush.

But back in Bonton, he was as ordinary as anybody else in that gym on Monday night. The floor had been divided into young black men there to play basketball and older white men there to help them understand that life on the streets was going to kill them.

"If you are really deciding to go with Jesus," Dad told the young men, "I will walk with you till Jesus comes."

"I felt as if he was speaking to me more than anyone else," Rodrick would later say. "My prayers were answered."

God started putting Rodrick's life back together. But his buddies were naturally skeptical about his newfound faith and about my father. *If this white man from North Dallas says Jesus is for real, why should we believe? And though he says he'll walk every step of the way with us, how do we know he actually will? We've been lied to before, mainly by chest-beating politicians who were there one day, making sound-bite promises on TV, and gone the next.*

Rodrick trusted my father. "He said I could call him anytime and he'd pray for me," Rodrick told his pals. "Day or night."

His friends looked at him. "OK, man, call him now. See if he'll pray for you right now."

Rodrick pulled out his cell phone and punched in the numbers.

"What's going on?" Rodrick said when my father answered.

"Hey, Rodrick," my dad said. "I'm, uh, at the White House right now. It's the National Day of Prayer."

"You at the White House? Well, I am sorry, I—"

"No, no, no, I can talk to you," said my dad. "You're my brother. I have to go pray, but let me pray for you first."

And right there, over the phone, my dad—in the same room as the most powerful leader in the free world, the president of the United States—prayed for a recovering Bonton drug dealer.

Rodrick was only slightly less stunned than the others. "The guy is genuine," he told them. "He's with the president of the United States. And he stops to pray with me."

Twenty-Six

THE ABUNDANT LIFE

:::::

Months later, at my dad's invitation, Rodrick took what must have been another huge leap of faith—going to a Prestonwood men's retreat. For most guys, going to a men's retreat is scary enough, even when you're going with guys you already know from church. Imagine a recovering drug dealer going to such a retreat when he'd hardly been in a church, period, and was now supposed to be confronting his life while thrown together with a bunch of guys he didn't know from wealthy North Dallas. That's courage, plain and simple.

When Rodrick heard the speaker talk about facing one's sin and letting God's grace put that sin behind you, he couldn't hold back the tears. Finally, he had to leave the room. What made him uncomfortable wasn't the fact that there were guys in the room who were so different from him. What made him uncomfortable was facing himself.

God was working on his heart. And my father's Bridge-Builder associate, Sharon Emmert, was working on getting him a job. That was how my dad rolled, with the realization that the gospel lived out must address not only someone's spiritual needs but their physical needs as well.

Dad wasn't big on theology or deep doctrinal discussions. He knew it intuitively. He had a deep understanding of what many would call the gospel of the kingdom—that the kingdom of God is relevant to your work, relationships, social structures, and more. It is relevant to all of life.

As my father feathered such thinking into his life and into the warp and woof of the BridgeBuilders ministry, Sharon was indispensable to Dad's work, a spark plug who could ream out folks with the passion of a drill sergeant but was fueled by a passion to see them succeed. "Valiant" is how my father described her.

"She loved the men and women of the ministry," he wrote. "If she was ever mad, she'd say, 'I'm going to put my pumps on.' We called her the Energizer Bunny. Here was this little white lady in her late fifties, and when she went down to Turner Courts, the most dangerous area of the hood, to help out, she was a woman on a mission. She kept a little office down there and just loved it. She held this ministry together."

Sharon and my dad wanted Rodrick to enroll in a work prep class that H.I.S. BridgeBuilders offered. Sharon called Rodrick. "Get over here and take this test," she said. He raced to get on the bus.

"She's four feet tall, she's white, man, she means business," he remembered. "If she tells me something, I better do it. I got to know her. As I got in the class, Sharon kind of kept me from getting off on the wrong track. She's sitting down having lunch with me, asking what I know about Southern cooking. She reads a devotional with me, gets me into a good study habit. Then Mike says, 'We need you in the community.' He wanted me to share my testimony. And I did. But I felt so disconnected from the Lord.

"I said to his associate, 'Josh, I asked the Lord to search my life and show me what I'm doing wrong, and what came up is that I'm shacking here with my baby's momma.'"

Josh suggested he talk to my dad, who said he would be happy to marry him and Lisa whenever they wanted. At first there was talk of having the ceremony in the small apartment they leased in the projects where they lived, but Rodrick sensed that his fiancée, Lisa, was hoping for something a bit nicer than that.

"Mike, I can't afford a wedding," he told my dad.

"You're my brother," my father said. "You're going to have a wedding. Have faith. We might be able to have it at Prestonwood."

"I definitely can't afford *that*!"

Rodrick and Lisa were married at the three-hundred-seat chapel at Prestonwood Baptist Church in Plano. "It was awesome to see the church step up to meet whatever needs arose for the wedding—making cakes, for example," my dad later wrote. Others helped with rings, dresses, tuxes, and so on. The church's wedding coordinator worked closely with them. The wedding was beautiful.

Sharon helped Rodrick get a job at the Lens Lab. A couple from Prestonwood found them a far better living arrangement, with new furniture donated by people in the church. And another couple from Prestonwood came alongside and mentored Rodrick and Lisa as they prepared to be married.

Rodrick was the first of Bonton young men who dared to

step forward—and out of the drug-dealing muck. His example, however, inspired Clifton Reese, who, like Rodrick, had had a hellacious childhood.

Clifton's father was a heroin addict. The family was dirt-poor. Ten boys. Brothers, cousins everywhere, but no adult male role models to be seen. As he was going through junior high, Clifton watched his stepfather beat his mother. He saw him drag her behind a truck for more than a block. And the stepfather routinely beat Clifton. Finally, he'd had enough. "I told him he was never whupping me again. I couldn't cry anymore. It was anger and hate. I hated him with a passion."

At seventeen, he left home to live the life of a drug dealer. Meanwhile, he ramped up his concern about his mother. "You touch her again and I'll kill you," he told his stepfather.

Clifton lived on the street, going from this girl's house to that girl's house. Stayed with aunts. He got married to SeAndra, and they were pregnant with a baby boy. As he got deeper into drug dealing, she had finally had it. "You need to choose drugs or your family," SeAndra told him.

Clifton chose drugs.

As with Rodrick, it was Velma Mitchell who planted the seed of his getting right with God. "Stop playing with your life," she told him. If Velma planted the seed, my father took over from there. Like Rodrick, Clifton made a commitment during a basketball event.

He not only connected with the heavenly Father out of the deal, but he found a new earthly father too—*my dad*. And a new brother—*me*.

Clifton wasted no time calling my dad just that: Dad. He'd never had one in any sense of the word. Never had a man in his life who cared whether he lived or died, much less cared that he lived the best life possible.

When my father saw Clifton's living conditions—he was living with a bunch of drug addicts—he all but grabbed Clifton and moved him out and into an apartment far from those guys.

What changes people? Not theology. Not adhering to rules and regulations. Not perfect church attendance. Here, ask Clifton.

"What changed my life," he said, "is a guy named Mike coming down and showing me how much he loved me."

Twenty-Seven

TWO-WAY STREET

:::::

After my junior year of high school, I had been interning at Turner Courts when I met Clifton. We started meeting together and vowed to set goals for our lives and keep each other accountable.

Initially, our meetings started out with me talking and him just looking at this white kid, like, "Dude, are you crazy? Are you really sitting here telling me I can get my life back together?" Over time, though, Clifton started dominating the meetings with stories of what God was doing in his life.

I loved it.

My goals had to do with making good grades and going to college—University of Texas, as it turned out. His had to do with earning his GED, getting optical training, and reuniting with his family. He told me he wanted to be a husband to his wife and a father to his children.

Our spiritual connection grew into a bona fide friendship. During my senior year of high school and the summer afterward, we met a couple of times a week. It wasn't just me encouraging him; it was him encouraging *me*. Iron sharpening iron, you know. It was the first time I'd had a brother pushing me. Teachers, parents, pastors, yes—but this was a friend. He made me serious about my faith because he was serious about his.

As I watched my father be a father to Clifton, I saw an amazing transformation in my new friend: He became like a new husband to his wife, SeAndra. He became like a new father to his son, Arnaz. Remember how Rodrick's son was emulating his dad in rolling a joint? Here was Arnaz, trying to be like Clifton, but in *good* ways. The little boy wanted to be just like his dad. He wanted to ride with his dad, shoot the ball like his dad, do everything like his dad. "Take me with you," he'd say. "I want to go with you." It was lots of fun seeing those two together.

Gradually, Clifton and Rodrick began sharing their newfound faith with guys like them in Bonton. Before, BridgeBuilders' Bible studies had mainly drawn older women. But now, slowly but surely, the ministry was reaching the community's key element—young men. My father's philosophy was simple: Changing young fathers like Clifton and Rodrick can change families. And changed families can revive an entire community.

As this shift occurred, Dad and Velma worked together less and less—he concentrating on discipling young men, and she on women. The two were still united in purpose, but it was as if a torch had been passed, and a new source of energy was helping drive the ministry.

When I left for college, Clifton and I stayed in touch by phone. What thrilled me was that you could see the spiritual progress he was making. It wasn't my relationship with Clifton that was carrying him; it was his relationship with Christ. He became the manager of the lens clinic where he trained. He started leading

Bible studies of his own. He ignited faith in other young men who'd otherwise be lost to the streets. He helped feed the homeless—a guy who, himself, was living out of his car only a few years before.

Then, during my sophomore year, I met Caitlin, the girl I would end up marrying. She immediately bonded with Clifton's wife, SeAndra. They became sisters in Christ. What made it really cool is that SeAndra is deaf and Caitlin just happened to be fluent in sign language. So that helped bring down barriers too. Caitlin helped SeAndra become more than she otherwise would have been, and SeAndra helped Caitlin do the same.

That's the thing about my father's story that I don't want overlooked: Folks from North Dallas investing in the folks from South Dallas was no one-way street.

It was never about us bursting into the lives of the people in Bonton and saying, in essence, *Hey, try to be like us. Try to be as good as us.* It was two groups of people committing to Christ and investing in *each other.* Two disparate—and in some ways *desperate*—groups of people using their friendship as leverage to try to be more like Jesus. And because of their oneness in him, seeing their differences melt like summer ice cream.

My dad said as much about me and Clifton: "The relationship I built with Velma Mitchell—Dad and Mom, some called us—ultimately allowed Clifton to have a life impact on my son. Faith without works is dead. Kids need a chance to serve. Kids with privilege need to see what it's like when someone's living on thirty-eight dollars a month, when they've got no place to live and no clothes to wear. Very few in the suburbs face this. But

Clifton allowed my son to not be shielded. Just like Jesus asked the disciples to walk with him and cross whatever cultural chasm came their way, so we need to do the same."

So, no, it wasn't about us inspiring them. It was a two-way street. Each of us helping the other. As time passed, the effort bore fruit in big ways—somebody homeless moving into a Habitat for Humanity house in Bonton. And sometimes in seemingly small ways that nevertheless spoke volumes. Like when Rodrick and Lisa Yarbrough went with my father on a mission trip to Romania sponsored by Prestonwood. In London, en route to Romania, Rodrick had bought a new pair of tennis shoes and a Dallas Cowboys hat. He was thrilled. Later, he was on a subway when he saw a young man wearing tattered shoes. Rodrick didn't even hesitate. The former drug dealer gave the young man his new hat and shoes on the spot. The lesson, my father would later relate, was straight from the Bible: "The man with the least had given the most."

Twenty-Eight

THE GREAT
ADVENTURE

::::

Some may have thought Sharon Emmert had no business being on those Bonton streets because she was from North Dallas and so darned refined. But there she was, not only encouraging others—*giving*—but benefiting from the experience herself. *Getting.*

"God is in Bonton," she would say.

She loved the place. She helped BridgeBuilders launch the optical clinic. Once or twice a week, opticians came to volunteer. And she helped start the dental clinic. She lived in North Dallas but rented a little apartment in the inner city just so she could be closer to the people.

When she learned she had cancer and perhaps not much time to live, she refused to let the prognosis stop her work in Bonton. She put pillows in her car so she'd be comfortable and had her daughter drive her around the hood. "Now, slow down, I need to talk to this person," she'd say, and she would encourage someone she knew on the street. OK, "encourage" with a touch of "command." "You need to go to GED class," she'd say. Or, "You need to get job training." Or, "You need to go to the clinic."

The last time Sharon was in Bonton, she was so tired that she spent the night at Velma Mitchell's house. Cancer doesn't bat last; God does. On Sharon's last night on earth, a candle-light vigil was held for her as we gathered to say good-bye—for now. People stood in her backyard in Plano. Her husband, Jim, opened the curtains so she could hear us as we sang songs of praise and prayed for her. People from Prestonwood. And people from Bonton who carpooled to get there, people who realized that her prodding never was about power but about her commitment to caring for them.

And then, just like that, she was gone. My father had now lost two good friends to cancer—E. K. Bailey and Sharon Emmert.

"We are creatures of comfort," my dad used to say. "We stay where we think the risk is the least, but it's a slow drift to destruction." Getting out of our comfort zones melds us with the true marrow of life God intends for us to find.

Sharon had learned that. Sharon had *lived* that. So did my father. In some ways, he believed comfort was an impediment to doing God's work. Not, of course, that he would count himself among "the uncomfortable"; goodness, we lived in a nice house in a nice neighborhood, and my siblings and I attended a private Christian school.

All of that, of course, cost money. At this point in my dad's life—he was forty-seven—a financial counselor probably would have recommended that he cut back on BridgeBuilders and press for a promotion at Prestonwood—or perhaps start a speaking ministry on the side to bring in extra income. Dad had fought the good fight for Bonton and beyond for more than a decade. He could easily rationalize simplifying his life and improving his bottom line.

But about midway through the first decade of the new millennium, Dad began going through yet another soul-searching stage. The issue was related to comfort. He had a great job and was financially secure. But quietly, he anguished over whether God really wanted him at Prestonwood. He had been there for nine years at that point, but he sensed that God was nudging him to leave. Then he'd think, *No, no, no. I can't leave Prestonwood.* He was tight with pastor Jack Graham and executive pastor Mike Buster. He'd helped build this church with his fund-raising prowess. People liked my father, and he liked them.

Then the tug to leave would return, and he'd repeat the soul-searching process. One weekend, I was home from college and staying up late to play an NCAA football video game when I heard Dad crying downstairs. He'd been praying alone, unaware that I was awake. He asked me to pray with him. I asked what was going on.

"I'm probably going to go with BridgeBuilders full-time," he said.

By then, we'd learned never to be too surprised by Dad's decisions. If anyone marched to his own drummer—to God's beat—it was him. And if that's what you're doing instead of marching to the cultural beat, you *have* to be making some surprising choices from time to time.

That said, the family, instead of responding with a group hug, shared a group cry when Dad—with Mom's blessing—later confirmed he was leaving Prestonwood. We were together in the car when he told us. Initially, my sister and brothers thought they'd need to leave Prestonwood Christian Academy—not the case, as it turned out. As we talked about it, we realized this is what my father felt God calling him to do.

"Dad, this is going to be a great adventure," said my younger brother, Jonathan, then fourteen. "Let's go."

Never mind that Dad and Mom had three kids still at home and one off-to-college kid whose yearly tab was in the $20,000 range. Never mind that he had made a $50,000 pledge to Prestonwood's capital campaign. He felt God was leading him to leave the megachurch—and a very nice salary—and go full-time with the poor. On top of this, he hadn't taken any salary from BridgeBuilders in the decade it had been operating, so now he would have to raise even more funds to compensate for his lost Prestonwood salary.

The thing that makes this such a God story is that my father, at his core, was about organization. He loved arranging pictures or flowers just right on a wall or shelf. When we had professional family photos taken, he insisted we all wear perfectly coordinated outfits. He liked things to be *neat*. And BridgeBuilders wasn't at all neat. Two diverse cultures such as North Dallas and Bonton mixing together wasn't neat; sometimes it meant a phone call in the middle of the night and hearing about a kid gunned down in the street. And now, giving up a good-paying job and trusting God would provide, well, that wasn't neat either.

But, my dad would tell us, that's what makes life such an adventure. "We hold on to our thimble," he would say. "God holds the ocean."

Twenty-Nine

THE SILENCE OF GOD

:::

If leaving Prestonwood in November 2008 seemed like just another expression of Dad's sense of urgency, something strange happened after he left, something I'd never seen before: He went into a yearlong funk.

At Prestonwood, he was part of a well-oiled machine with seemingly unlimited resources at his fingertips. That wasn't the case with BridgeBuilders, which survived on prayer, persistence, and good intentions. The BridgeBuilders phone all but stopped ringing. Donations slowed to a trickle.

"No one was listening," wrote my father. "I was walking with God, and yet there seemed to be no favor of God. God went quiet."

The office he had moved into was uninspiring and cramped—just Dad, Mary, and occasionally my mother, hardly the parade of people who'd come through his office at Prestonwood. He was walking the tightrope of depression. "It was a very dark season for Mike," said my mother.

The lull started to eat at my father. "I can't do this anymore," he wrote. "I give up. If you want this ministry to succeed, then, God, you need to move any way you want."

There was no immediate lightning bolt. No voice from the heavens. I suggested that Dad start a blog to help raise awareness and support for the ministry. But he wasn't exactly computer savvy. Despite that, he reluctantly started a blog. A grand total of thirty people subscribed to his daily messages. *Thirty.* That only added insult to injury.

Losing Sharon was contributing to his downcast mood too. She had been not only a friend and fellow soldier in the trenches, but a competent compatriot who sharpened him, the ministry's fund-raising efforts, and the Cliftons of the world who needed love-based prodding.

"After Sharon died, BridgeBuilders lost a lot of momentum," said Mary Anderwald, who became Dad's assistant when he left Prestonwood.

He grew concerned about making payroll for the dozen employees; my dad, of course, wasn't taking a salary. So he began making plans to sell our house, give the equity to pay off a $50,000 Prestonwood pledge, and pump some cash into BridgeBuilders.

But Mary had been praying fervently; Dad called her his "blessed intercessor." And God was quietly at work. Indeed, if my father's life journey had, for the first time, slowed to a Mississippi-mud pace, rapids awaited—followed by a waterfall none of us expected.

In early 2009, my mother and father went to the White House

Office of Faith-Based and Community Initiatives (OFBCI) conference in Dallas.

One of the speakers, Michael Simpson, impressed my folks. He was a South Dallas kid who'd risen from the BridgeBuilders program that my dad and mom and Velma had begun.

"We saw him up there and said, 'That's our guy, the fruit of our labor,'" said my mom. It was as if my parents were stepping back and seeing the incredible reach of the ministry's work. The benefits weren't just a guy like Clifton getting out of the drug wars and into God's grace; they stretched farther and wider than they'd imagined. From a simple Bible study Dad and Velma had started, the poor were now being ministered to in Bonton, San Antonio, and Clarksburg, West Virginia, places where BridgeBuilders branch ministries operated. Progress *was* being made. Lives *were* being changed.

Beyond that, Michael Simpson was saying things about ministry structure that my dad needed to hear. BridgeBuilders had always been a seat-of-the-pants ministry, a reflection of my father's "pray and God will provide" approach to life. But the ministry had grown so large that it threatened to implode without more structure, direction, and energy beyond what Dad and a few others could offer. What's more, it needed a serious cash infusion.

My dad pulled out a napkin during Simpson's talk and started sketching a business model that integrated BridgeBuilders with a handful of other nonprofits, from the Urban League to homeless shelters to the Dallas Housing Authority—various ways for clients to be fed into the ministry. Instead of seeing BridgeBuilders as operating in some sort of vacuum, he began realizing it could best thrive as one step in a larger process that involved other organizations.

From the Salvation Army to community colleges to the Boys & Girls Clubs of America, a dozen or so entities could feed people into BridgeBuilders. The organization would help educate, train, and mentor people. From there, others—churches, Habit for Humanity, microbusinesses, and more—would get involved to help complete the process of helping individuals rebuild their lives.

"Initially, with BridgeBuilders, Mike was all about prayer, Bible study, evangelism, maybe GED, and a little job training if someone else would run it," said my mom. "All great things, but structure and a focused plan were needed. The conference helped him to see that."

Dad loved his flowchart; you'd have thought he invented the wheel. But the cool thing was it helped to get him back on track, to envision a new future, and to renew his sense of purpose with BridgeBuilders.

So did some other changes. Back home, a couple of well-to-do women from Prestonwood, Kathi Yeager and Judy Burleson, invited my father to use offices they had—offices far more inspiring and effective than the one that Dad and company had been using. Kathi, it turns out, was a marketing expert, and at Dad's request, she rolled up her sleeves to write a strategic plan for the ministry.

It was all very exciting—flowcharts, business models, the works. Kathi helped Dad craft a mission statement for BridgeBuilders: "H.I.S. BridgeBuilders is a movement of God uniting Christians across cities to restore urban communities through education, health, economic, and spiritual development."

But just when my dad was starting to appear almost conventional—a businessman with Jesus' heart and actual *focus*—he reminded us all that he was, after all, Mike Fechner, never totally predictable.

Thirty

A TWINGE OF PAIN

:::::

"I'm going to Romania," he told us out of the blue. He wanted to encourage pastors there and help the poor.

A few years earlier, he had gone to Brazil with Johnson Ellis, a North Dallas friend who is actively involved with a missionary organization that ministers along the Amazon River. For a guy most comfortable at Nordstrom, that was as far out of my dad's comfort zone as he'd ever been. My dad hated to fly, much less muck around in a jungle. But Dad made the trip, and earlier, as Prestonwood's minister of global outreach, he had traveled to Romania. He went as part of a U.S. team whose goal was to meet with and encourage Romanian pastors. Now he was headed back to eastern Europe.

"All of these pastors think we're the 'Great American Church' coming over to help them build their churches," he wrote. "But I challenged them to pray for and help each other so they could build each other up. Together, in prayer, they could do more than what we could by bringing them a dollar or two from the United States."

The team's effort triggered a new "pastors conference" concept to bring churches in Romania together to help one another, which was all fine and good in my father's eyes. But he was far more interested in Romania's gypsies, the lepers of their time and place.

When he first saw these people, he told the pastors he wanted to meet with the poor. "No, no, no," they said. "Those are the gypsies. They're dangerous. The Valley of Galati [Romania] was just like South Dallas, and the church has evacuated this area in much the same way the church has abandoned Bonton before the Lord led us there," Dad wrote. "I get this. I know what it means to feel alone and rejected. I'd seen it in Bonton."

Communism, he believed, had long since robbed the people of any sense of self-worth. "There was nothing unique or distinctive about you. There was no Jesus who had a purpose and a plan for your life. You conform. You're under complete authority. You're a robot. Creativity and entrepreneurship had been taken away. It was a wasteland of dreariness."

My father, of course, loved it—not the place, but the challenge, the people, the opportunity for God to do a work there. Now he was going back to Romania, not on behalf of Prestonwood to encourage pastors, but on behalf of Jesus, through BridgeBuilders, to bring hope to people at the street level. It was at the street level where girls between the ages of thirteen and eighteen were seldom seen because they'd been sold into the sex industry and shipped to other countries.

He remembered a little girl he'd seen on his first trip. "This beautiful little child was looking at me—this little girl scooping up dirt and putting it in her mouth as if it were food," he wrote. "I thought, *That child is eating dirt.* She was emaciated and hungry, but when I pointed it out to a missionary from the U.S., he said, 'We don't have time to meet all the needs. We're just preaching the gospel.' And I said, 'That *is* the gospel. The gospel is word and deed. You must feed these people; you must figure that out. That's God's child. You read the Scripture tonight and tell me tomorrow where it says we can ignore the child eating dirt.'" The next day, the missionary returned to Dad. Broken and repentant, he pledged to help meet the needs of the people, both spiritual and physical.

Dad had built a long-distance relationship with a gypsy pastor named Bogdon Mihai. He wanted to look into working with Mihai to disciple people and to open an optical clinic and lab to train the poor so they could find jobs. Whether it was across town or across the world, he needed to be looking people in the eye, praying with them, and seeing to it that they had food instead of dirt.

It was the spring of 2009, about four or five months after Dad had left his job at Prestonwood. The funk was over. The idea of returning to Romania fired Dad up. Life was good.

Then he felt the pain in his stomach.

He had been blow-drying his hair in the bathroom. Mom was brushing her teeth. When she finished, Dad said the first words that began to describe a life-changing experience: "This kind of keeps hurting."

The doctor said it was probably his gallbladder. Scans were done. "Yes, let's take out the gallbladder," a doctor said. The surgery was done—the first time my always-healthy father had experienced an overnight stay in a hospital. When the surgery was over, the doctor said it was successful.

Then, why, wondered my dad later, *did my stomach still hurt?*

Thirty-One

THE BOMB

::::

A few months later, my father was praying early one morning when he sensed God telling him to get another scan. *This shouldn't still be hurting,* he thought. So he went in for a CT scan.

The technicians slid him into that giant donut hole. It was scary. But not as scary as the waiting. The doctor called the next day. "I have the results," he said.

It was morning. My father was in the bedroom, getting ready. "Well, good," my father said. *It was no big deal, right?*

There was a pause on the other end of the line. "Well, everything looks fine in the abdomen area," the doctor said. "It's diverticulitis. That's what the pain was there, and we can control that by diet"—*Whew,* my father sighed—"but the scan went higher than the abdomen to the bottom of your lungs. We've seen a mass there, and it appears you have lung cancer. And you'll need to have further tests done. I can recommend some doctors."

I told you in the beginning that my father was human. That, as sold as he was on Jesus, he had his moments. And so his initial reaction to this news was a human reaction, the way you'd expect any one of us to react: He thought God was playing some sort of bad joke on him. Why this when he was just getting momentum back doing God's work? He muttered "thank you" into the phone, hung up, walked into the bathroom, and wept.

"It was like a bomb went off in my mind, my heart, my head," he later wrote. "I couldn't rationally think what to do. Here I am, forty-seven, doing ministry, doing the right thing, trying to follow God. And now I have lung cancer?

"It didn't seem fair. Why couldn't the universe give this disease to a mass murderer or a megalomaniacal dictator? Why me? After all I had been through, after all I had learned about faith and ministry, dying from cancer felt like a tragic waste of life experience."

Nothing was conclusive yet. The doctor said "it appears" that Dad had lung cancer. But couldn't the doctor be wrong?

"We just need to get this tested out," my mom told him. "Let's pray it's not cancer."

Dad called Mike Buster. "Mike," he told my dad, "there's no way you could have lung cancer. You don't even smoke." (A common misconception, this.)

It was terminal. The doctor, a man of East Indian descent, was confident, articulate, and to the point. "You have eight to eighteen months to live," he told my father at Baylor University Medical Center. "There is no cure." This was July 1, 2009.

Stage 4 lung cancer. Technically, *adenocarcinoma.*

God whispered something deeper to my father: *You aren't terminal. You are eternal.*

"We can give you an oral chemo that will slow things down,"

the doctor said, "but the cancer will grow around it, and after that point, there's nothing we can do."

My father glanced across the small office, where he saw a magazine featuring Christmas on its cover. This was summer. My father's mind fast-forwarded to Christmas, a season he loved. Six months away. Would he see another Christmas with us, his family? If he did, would it be his last?

Romon Mitchell, Velma's son.

E. K. Bailey, Dad's close friend and mentor.

Sharon Emmert, his right-hand woman in BridgeBuilders.

Like his three friends, my father had apparently been accepted into a death club to which he did not want a membership.

It's interesting, my father said, what your mind gravitates to when you hear you are soon going to die. In his case, it was the lament of perhaps no more Christmases with the family.

I was headed home from Austin—my girlfriend, Caitlin, and sister, Grace, were with me—when I got the call. Dad told me he needed to talk to me alone so I exited the freeway, and while the girls were getting drinks, I called him back.

"You alone?" he asked.

"Yeah," I said. *What was going on? Some sort of surprise party?*

"The doctors called," he said. His voice was weak and trembling; I'd never heard him like that. "I have lung cancer."

The exchange was surreal. We didn't talk long. I just said we'd fight this; we'd figure it out. All the years I'd come to him with this challenge or that. In that moment, it almost seemed like role reversal. As if, at twenty-one, I was the father, the one who needed to be strong and have all the answers.

By the time we got to Dallas, I was already getting calls and text messages from friends who'd heard the news. When people at Prestonwood and in Bonton heard the news, word spread fast. People were already praying for my father.

Once home, Dad gathered the family—the children he would later describe like this: "Grace, twelve. The little girl we'd always prayed for. My blue-eyed princess. Loud and fun and a leader. On the swim team; Jonathan, fourteen. Sandy-haired. Joy boy. Wakes up happy. Loves people. Loves God. Always makes us laugh; Daniel, eighteen. High school senior. Football player. Good-looking kid. Strong convictions. Hard-driving leader; Michael, twenty-one. Student at University of Texas. Political aspirations. Big, strapping football player, all-state in high school. Born leader. Big guy. One of my heroes."

He told us he had cancer, though offered none of the "eight months to eighteen months" details. He told us we were going to trust God on this one. Then he told us we were all going to the Cheesecake Factory, his favorite restaurant.

"We're going to have a party," he said, "to celebrate life." And we did.

Later, my little brother, Jonathan, came to my father. "Dad," he said, "you got to make it through Grace's senior year. She needs you."

She wasn't even a teenager yet.

"So, is that all I'm going to need to make it through?" my dad asked Jonathan.

"You just need to make it that far," he said. "She needs you that far."

Thirty-Two

QUESTIONS FOR GOD

::::

The next day, my father lounged out in the pool, making calls, going about his business, almost as if by ignoring the specter it would go away. As if he could *will* it away

His July 8, 2009, blog entry was headlined "Detour Ahead." He spent the first paragraph mentioning that, oh, by the way, he had cancer and was now "going down a path that is unknown and uncertain." He spent the rest of the entry talking about the great needs in Romania. About how BridgeBuilders planned to partner with a Dallas businessman who wanted to move a tool and die plant to the country. About how he had planned to go back to Romania.

"Those were my plans for the week, but God has placed us on another path to seek healing," he wrote. "We thank God for his sovereignty and that we are to be anxious for nothing but pray about all things with thanksgiving" (Philippians 4:6).

Then, as the weeks unfolded, it sunk in: He was a self-described "dead man walking." The platitudes he'd heard from some people began grating on him like fingernails on a chalkboard: "Death is a natural part of life." "All of us will die someday; you just happen to know when." "God knows how special you are because you're strong enough to handle this." And, of course, "God works everything for good."

"Fine," he'd want to respond, "but you're not the one who's dying."

He knew there was truth in all the statements, but it wasn't helping him. He watched himself spin through Elisabeth Kübler-Ross's stages of grief with sickening randomness. "I found myself cycling through denial, anger, bargaining, depression, and then landing on acceptance all too briefly before whirling around again to denial."

He was angry with people and angry with God. He felt like a kid who diligently brushed his teeth, only to be told by a dentist that he had a mouthful of cavities. "I was, after all, a good man by most people's standards," he wrote. "I conducted business honestly. I attended church regularly. I gave a large portion of my wealth to charity. Without reservation, I shared my faith with those willing to hear me. I loved a good wife and reared honest children. At one point, I even sold my business and gave away much of my wealth to serve God in full-time ministry. I deserved to be healthy, wealthy, and fulfilled, not consumed from the inside by cancer."

My father wasn't proud of these feelings. He knew they mirrored a sense of entitlement that had been more common in the old Mike than the new. "But I have to be honest. Patients facing the fickle cruelty of death by disease eventually ask these questions. Even before given an expiration date, everyone struggles to make sense of a world that allows good people to suffer while bad people prosper."

Over the next few months, he tried to make sense of his feelings, God's promises, the whole nine yards. He began a dialogue with God. He didn't hear an audible voice, but based on Scripture, he said the conversation mirrored this:

> **Mike:** *Lord, why have you allowed cancer to invade my body? I thought you were looking out for me.*
>
> **God:** I allowed my Son to suffer. Are you, his servant, greater than he, your Master?
>
> **Mike:** *But Jesus suffered as part of your plan to redeem people from their sin and the world from the rule of evil.*
>
> **God:** Did he not call you to follow him and to become part of this plan?
>
> **Mike:** *Yes, but . . . I didn't know how much it would cost or how much it would hurt. I'm afraid, and I feel alone.*
>
> **God:** I am with you. My grace is sufficient to see you through this, and you will find my strength in your weakness. You must believe me when I say, *Don't be afraid.*
>
> **Mike:** *I have already given much, Lord. My career and my business. All my money. All my time. Even my family; I've surrendered my family to you. How much more do you want?*
>
> **God:** I want it all, Michael. I already owned everything you surrendered. I already own everything you have

not yet released. I want you to give me everything so you can be like my Son.

Mike: *Who suffered and died . . . unjustly.*

God: Yes. And then received glory that far outweighed his momentary suffering. When you follow his example—and you will, for I have ordained it so—I will not merely reward you; I will give you complete access to everything that is mine.

Mike: *I don't want to die.*

God: You must surrender your life to me.

Mike: *And if I surrender my life, will you cure my cancer?*

God: When you truly surrender your life to me, you will not need to know the answer. Then you will have become a true disciple, a full partner in my plan to redeem people from their sin and the world from the rule of evil. Surrender your life to me, Michael.

Mike: *I surrender it. Just give me mercy through the pain, and strength to finish well, and grace to make my last days count for Christ.*

God: I love you, my son.

Thirty-Three

THE RESURGENCE

::::

The news leveled everyone, including Dad's assistant, Mary. "Mike had become like a son to me," she said.

Velma's reaction to his prognosis mirrored how my father would want her to react. "I wanted to take his cancer away, but I can't do that," she said. "But the one thing I can do, I can love Jesus; I can love his people; I can teach them how much Jesus loves them. We can build a neighborhood that will bring people back to Jesus. As God told David, 'Get up, take back what's yours.'"

By the fall of 2009, my father was fairly resigned to the idea that he had no more than a year and a half to live. He'd gone through anger and denial and had reached acceptance. He planned his funeral, arranged his affairs, and prepared to die.

My mother, however, did not share his resignation. "I knew God wasn't done with him yet," she said. And, slowly, my father developed a similar resolve. Remembering E. K. Bailey's suggestion not to place your trust in conventional medicine, my folks started researching alternatives. They explored what other countries might offer, things that might be done to prolong, or save, my dad's life. While they did that, friends and neighbors were praying for them, bringing them meals, asking how else they could help.

"When asking what you can do for us," my father wrote in his July 31, 2009, blog entry, "the simple answer is to love the lost and least the way you love us."

The daily blog entries fell into a pattern: a quick update on Dad's condition, then a mention of something that had happened in my dad's life that glorified God—say, the lab team at Sammons Cancer Center at Baylor breaking out into song after Dad asked if the technicians knew any good praise hymns—and an update on H.I.S. BridgeBuilders.

He sang the praises of E. K. Bailey's replacement, Pastor Bryan Carter, and the "amazing" congregation of Concord Missionary Baptist Church. Spoke of the joy of learning that a local tool and die shop had hired five recent graduates of BridgeBuilders' machine shop skills training class. And printed the letter from my brother Jonathan about how someday he hoped to take over for my father as president of BridgeBuilders.

As Dad's bout with cancer deepened—chemo treatments had become part of his weekly routine—he turned, even more passionately, to those around him. "There are few things that could have been lower on my priorities in the past than to go to the hospital to visit the sick," he wrote. "But God has broken my hard heart. The Lord has broken my heart for the sick and hopeless."

He would walk up to complete strangers and ask them to share their stories with him. *Why are you in the hospital? How are you doing?* And harking back to his lessons from E. K.: *How can I help? How can I pray for you?*

Meanwhile, as he shared on his blog about cancer, BridgeBuilders, and the Lord, something amazing happened: He went from having a few dozen subscribers to more than seven thousand almost overnight. Yes, seven thousand. People were praying for him. People were donating to BridgeBuilders in his honor. People were rededicating their lives to Christ or bowing to him for the first time.

Dad's cancer had sparked a whole new level of giving, even if he wasn't particularly bold or persistent in asking for money. Dad had friends in high places. Dad had friends in low places. Dad had friends everywhere: An oil guy gave because my dad had become his friend—truly a friend, not someone who feigned friendship in an attempt to get a donation. Guys he'd discipled gave. Guys who he'd been there for when *they* were struggling gave.

BridgeBuilders volunteers came out of the woodwork. What's more, people stopped my dad in restaurants and on the street to pray with him. A dead-in-the-water deal to establish an economic development center for BridgeBuilders suddenly got legs.

Dad remembered what his mentor, the late pastor E. K. Bailey, taught him—that the greatest tragedies and hurts come into our lives so we might minister to others. Having cancer provided him with a greater platform and more influence than he ever dreamed of. With cancer, when he spoke to the residents of Bonton, he could more fully empathize with their plights and understand what it was like to experience pain and suffering. With cancer, when he spoke to wealthy Christians on behalf of his ministry, he could show them what true faith is—that it's not just something reserved for the good times, but it's for *all* times.

Likewise, he believed our attention should be reserved for other people and not for ourselves. "There were no 'random people' in the guy's life," said a friend, Chris Tedford.

In October 2009, Tedford and my dad were part of a small team of people that visited an official with the Department of Housing and Urban Development. While in Washington, D.C., the group also went to the National Mall. Clifton Reese was taking pictures, recalled Tedford. Bryan Carter, E. K.'s replacement, was checking out the Lincoln Memorial. And there was my father, tired because of the cancer, lying on a bench, spent— yet encouraging a homeless guy next to him.

"How can we pray for you?" he asked him.

Thirty-Four

SEARCHING FOR
ZACCHAEUS

:::::

Hope rose about a surgery that might be done on my father. The son-in-law of a Prestonwood member was a thoracic oncologist at Cedars-Sinai Medical Center in Los Angeles. After studying my father's biopsies and medical records, the doctor determined that surgery might, in fact, be an option.

In late October, my folks and Mike Buster flew to Los Angeles to meet with the doctor. However, further testing revealed more cancer in the lungs. Surgery, at least for now, was not a viable option.

My mother and Mike Buster were deflated, tired, and anxious to get back to the hotel and rest. My father's mind was on something different.

"Question," he said. "Where is the worst part of Los Angeles?"

"What?" said Buster.

"Where's LA's 'Bonton'?" he asked.

Buster frowned. "Well, I suppose Watts, but why do you—"

155

"Hop in," he said, pointing to the rental car. "Let's go to Watts."

"But, Mike, there's traffic; we're all tired."

Mom's face morphed into one of those "you've got to be kidding me" looks.

"Come on," said my dad, "let's go."

"But, Mike, it's going to be dark soon," she said. "We—"

"I'll drive."

And so my dad dragged Mike Buster and my mom to Watts. The housing development they arrived at looked like a prison.

"It was horrible, worse than Bonton before it got cleaned up," said Buster. "Rundown apartments. Winos. Drug dealers."

My mom, who wasn't about to leave the car, didn't like this scene at all. "You'd better not go out there," she said.

"What are they going to do to me?" my dad said. "I've already been cut open. I'm already on drugs. There's nothing they can do to me."

My dad opened the car door and walked over to a group of young guys who looked to be gang members.

Mike Buster also got out, locked the car (with Mom inside), and followed my dad.

"The guys on the street all thought we were cops," said Buster. "But there's Mike going up to these guys and saying, 'So, what's your biggest need? How can we help you solve this neighborhood's issues?' Some were obviously high, some drunk, some hoping they could sell us some drugs. But Mike just stood there for forty-five minutes, talking to ten to twelve of these guys. And, before I know it, we're all holding hands and praying. That was Mike Fechner."

The kicker: It wasn't even my father who began the prayer. It was the gang leaders themselves. My dad had inspired them that much.

Looking back on the incident, Buster just shook his head. "That guy was a man of prayer," he said. "Mike, better than anyone I know, adhered to the 'pray without ceasing' verse in the Bible. Drug dealers. Waitresses. Fellow hospital patients. Anywhere. Anytime. And he'd always tell you, 'That's what Jesus did. Everywhere he went, Jesus touched people. He looked for needs. Remember Zacchaeus, up in that tree? Nobody bothered looking up there, but Jesus did.'"

Caitlin, whom I'd been dating for only a few months at the time, remembers how quickly she and my father bonded—after an embarrassing "meet the parents" moment in which we arrived in Dallas from Austin late one night and set off the home security alarm. Mom and Dad had been asleep for hours and were in their pajamas.

"Two weeks after that, I went to Spain," she said. "While I was there, Father's Day rolled around. I'd lost my dad just a few years before, when I was eighteen. And I get this e-mail from Michael's dad, and he's telling me how he loves me like his own daughter. It was just so purposeful and heartfelt."

The most difficult year of my father's life was coming to an end—a year in which he learned he was likely to die soon—and what was he writing about on his blog? About how Clifton and SeAndra Reese and another person transformed through BridgeBuilders, Carla Robinson, were moving into their new Habitat for Humanity homes. How he and the rest of us in his family would, as usual, be in Bonton Christmas afternoon for the annual Christmas dinner, a $15,000-a-year endeavor that he hoped some of his blog readers might help support. (They did, big-time.) And how excited he was to be going with my brother Jonathan and me to Germany and Romania in January—the former country in order to receive treatment, the latter for ministry.

In the Valley of Galati, Romania, I met Bogdon Mihai, the "city pastor" as my father called him. His life had once been in shambles. He had sold drugs and run a prostitution ring. Three times he'd tried to commit suicide, but his life had been changed by the power of Christ.

In snow and freezing temperatures, we went to homes where twelve people might be living in two rooms. Using donations of money from people in Dallas, we delivered food, clothing, and firewood to the poor. And one family in particular was included.

My father had never forgotten the little girl eating dirt.

Thirty-Five

THE GIFT OF BREATH

:::::

Once we returned home from Europe, Dad trashed his junk-food ways and, on the advice of the German doctors, started eating an almost paleo-like diet—veggies, chicken, tea, and water mostly. The eight-month mark since the doctor told him he had "eight months to eighteen months to live" came and went. Tests showed that my father's two tumors had rapidly decreased in size, perhaps because of the shots he was taking on the advice of a German doctor. I believe it was due, at least in part, to the answered prayers of thousands.

In May 2010, I graduated from the University of Texas. Clifton and SeAndra joined Caitlin and my family for the ceremony. Afterward, my father bragged us up in a blog post. He wrote that he was honored that Clifton, one of the first men to catch the BridgeBuilders vision, would come all the way from Dallas to Austin for the event. Of me, he wrote that he was "honored to be his father and can truly say he is one of my heroes" (gulp)—and, of course, how thankful he was for "Christ, who strengthens us."

As summer turned to fall, my dad performed the ceremony

159

as Caitlin and I got married. He also pulled some strings to get former NFL placekicker and TV broadcaster Pat Summerall to share his testimony with recent graduates of H.I.S. Bridge-Builders employment training classes. And he welcomed me aboard as the head of the BridgeBuilders mentoring program, though I also had my eye on launching a business that would employ some of the Bonton guys.

Dad returned to Germany for more treatment and later flew to Los Angeles to have a surgeon remove a wedge from his lung. In a few weeks, February 3, 2011, my father would turn fifty. It had been eighteen months since a doctor had told him that, in the best case scenario, he'd be dead by now.

In his blog, Dad rejoiced about two things: that it appeared he was cancer-free and that he was going back to Los Angeles to help bring God's hope to the hopeless in Watts. "God's timing," he said, "is perfect."

Dad's bout with cancer unlocked a deeper eloquence within him. "How tragic it is," he wrote in the summer of 2011, "to spend our lives focusing on such small subjects as ourselves. I continue to be convicted by the amount of need globally and the excess locally."

With such clarity of thought, it's no wonder he had started to put together ideas and sample chapters for a book he hoped to write. And with his future all the more uncertain, he became even more intent on living for every moment. "Every breath," he wrote, "is a gift. Every inhalation a promise."

He was fearless in his outreach. In 2011, he took a friend, Kevin O'Neal, to Chattanooga, Tennessee, ostensibly to raise money for BridgeBuilders. But once there, Dad did almost exactly what he'd done with Mike Buster in Los Angeles. He "kidnapped" Kevin and took him to the poorest part of the city to talk to the poor.

"He was just so bold," said O'Neal. "The hosts were saying, 'You can't go here. You can't do this. There are gangs.' But he went anyway."

"There was a crazy beauty to the season of cancer with him," said another friend, Johnson Ellis, with whom my dad had gone to the Amazon. "It was always, 'I'm going to give my all to this.' There were never any safety nets for Mike Fechner."

For years, he'd been praying to start a church in South Dallas as part of the BridgeBuilders ministry. Now, one of his oil money connections stepped up to help BridgeBuilders lease a huge Dallas Housing Authority property in West Dallas. Not only was it perfect for an economic development center, but its warehouse would be well suited for a church.

This warehouse would provide a larger venue for employment training and for employment placement services. It also allowed the staff to be together at one location. In 2011, Dad reveled in the opening of BridgeBuilders' 62,000-square-foot Economic Development Center. And later, he beamed when the first service was held at the new Restoration Community Church, where Dad, the self-described "white guy from Plano," served as copastor with Von Minor, a black pastor formerly with Oak Cliff Bible Fellowship.

On that first Sunday, Dad's eyes glistened as he stood at the podium and looked at the few hundred people present. Among those who had shown up? His mom and dad, who had come all the way from San Antonio to surprise him.

Thirty-Six

FRUIT OF THE LABOR

:::::

Everywhere he looked, my father was seeing God at work in the lives of those in Bonton and those at Prestonwood. His cancer was behaving itself, and his God was doing great things in the lives of people he loved. People such as:

- Hector, a Hispanic man who came to BridgeBuilders on the recommendation of his probation officer. He was a two-time convicted felon and drug dealer who'd come to know Christ in prison. But he was homeless when he showed up at BridgeBuilders. Then, a transformation: He completed the BridgeBuilders job-training program, became a promising leader, and soon was named supervisor of our solar screen business while mentoring five young men in the community.

- The folks in Bonton who insisted on raising a tent in a field full of sandburs on the Fourth of July to hold a freedom fest of sorts—the freedom afforded by our country and the freedom afforded us through Christ. Folks still tell the story about a woman driving on a nearby highway who heard the music and wondered what was going on in Bonton. She stopped, and when she saw what was happening, she came forward to rededicate her life to Christ.

- The wealthy guy from Plano whom my father encouraged to check out Bonton to see what BridgeBuilders was doing there. Daron Babcock was a vice president of sales for a huge corporation. He was so impressed that he prayed a courageous prayer: *God, I'll do whatever you want me to.* The answer he discerned was this: *Sell your house and move to Bonton.* As he readied to make the move, he was looking for a fun way to build a relationship with the young men of Bonton, so he invited them to his house for lunch, picked them up in two Hummer limos, and hired a Christian rapper to provide inspiration.

- The Plano family, as part of a North Dallas/South Dallas partnership sponsored by BridgeBuilders, that befriended a Bonton teenager who was in danger of getting sucked into a gang. Then family members offered to pay for the teen's college education.

- The young couple my father had discipled in an evening class held in our home years before. Now they were heading off to New York City, leaving their comfortable home in North Dallas to live in a 600-square-foot apartment in Harlem to be trained in church planting while ministering to international students at Columbia University.

BridgeBuilders was working both ways, just as my father had dreamed. High-profile business types had quit their jobs, taken pay cuts, and gone to work for the ministry. A savvy group of business executives had helped take the ministry to the next level. It was now thriving in five cities: Dallas; San Antonio; Clarksburg, West Virginia; Buffalo; and Galati, Romania.

The new church, Restoration Community, was alive and growing. Each year, BridgeBuilders' Optical Clinic was providing low-cost vision care to approximately 7,000 patients, dispensing some 2,500 pairs of lenses. Every second Saturday, hundreds of volunteers were coming to Bonton to feed the poor and to help the elderly and disabled with lawn care and landscaping and picking up trash, and—most importantly in my father's eyes—to build relationships.

But if all these things looked good on the ministry's website, it was the face-to-face stuff that stoked my father's emotional fires. It wasn't the awards he'd been given—from the Zig Ziglar Servant Leadership Award to the Let Justice Roll on Like a River award from the Foundation for Community Empowerment. It wasn't the prestige of sitting on boards such as the Dallas-area Habitat for Humanity or having been given an honorary doctorate from Carver Bible College.

What excited him was changed lives, as was seen when BridgeBuilders celebrated the first graduating class from its Omni Hotel training class. Wrote one of the grads, "I truly feel part of something special, and I know it is not my doing, but God's."

If Dad loved the poor and downtrodden, he loathed how some people from outside Bonton were quick to judge them.

"Please do not judge the reason the poor are in the position they are in until you have walked among them," he wrote in a December 2011 blog post. "Jesus seldom spoke a harsh word to the poor or afflicted, but often spoke harshly to the Pharisees, who thought they were guides to the blind and yet were blind to Jesus and his gospel."

On the other hand, he loved givers who went above and beyond. A friend of my father's from Austin called just before the holidays. "What do you need for your Bonton kids for Christmas, Mike?" he asked.

My father threw out a number, leaning toward the high end because he knew his friend had plenty to give. "Great," the man said. "Let's do ten times that. The check will be there tomorrow."

More than a thousand people from South Dallas showed up in Bonton on Christmas Day. Three hundred people had volunteered to help. Seven people made a profession of faith in Christ.

Thirty-Seven

COMPASSION IN KENYA

My father was still on a high when he stepped onto a plane in early January 2012 to fly to Nairobi, Kenya. He had been told two and a half years earlier that his life was soon going to end. But when given the opportunity to explore another needy place far from home, he quickly said yes—and invited my brother Daniel, then twenty, to join a group that also included Dad's friend Johnson Ellis.

In some ways, the poverty and hopelessness in Nairobi made Romania look tame. The average home, he found, was ten feet by twelve feet, and five people might live in that space. Raw sewage ran openly through the streets. HIV was spreading and claiming the lives of innocent children every day—fully 6 percent of the population.

"Yet in all this hopelessness, Jesus is more than enough," he wrote. "The faith of so many of the Kenyans in these horrific conditions is humbling. I must confess that I am undone by their godliness and contentment. We asked one of the women in one of the worst slums what her dream was for her life, and she answered, 'To lead more people to God.' Not a new home, a new car, a new flat-screen TV, or even to get out of the slums, but to lead others to Christ. They represent 'count it all joy' more powerfully than any group of people I've ever seen."

The Nairobi slums had their own Mother Teresa, known as Mama Lucy. At a time when thugs were stealing and looting and raping women, Mama Lucy would pray, "Help me love my neighbors more than myself." She gave gifts to others and encouraged young people to do good, not evil. The leader of a gang heard about this and put his face in hers.

"You are a *crazy* lady," he said. "I will *kill* you."

Then one of his gang buddies was hurt badly. Mama Lucy paid for the injured man to go to the hospital. Later, the young man who had threatened her was badly beaten for breaking into someone's home. He was taken to the morgue, along with the bodies of two thugs. The next morning he "came to," as if he'd risen from the dead. When he opened his eyes, there was Mama Lucy, ready to walk with him and pay for his recovery in the hospital. The young man gave his life to Jesus on the spot.

Johnson Ellis remembers the slums as an absolute feeding ground for infection. "I've never seen such filth," he said. "But there was this lady sitting there, dying, and even though Mike was feeling sick himself, he carried that woman out so she could sit in the sun with her grandchildren. He caressed her shoulder and prayed for her, even though most of us were thinking, *You touch that lady, and you're going to get AIDS.* When we got home, he sent money to her family for sheets and mattresses and so they could be relocated. He had this crazy, beautiful way with people."

"Dad loved to talk about the kingdom, and going to Kenya with him taught me more about the kingdom," said my brother Daniel. "So many of our brothers and sisters with far less material stuff than we have in America have so much more joy. They treasure God. They experience him as Provider, Healer, Sustainer.

"Like Dad, I've always liked nice things too much, so he probably chose me to go with him to the slums for a reason. I still remember our plane ride home: 'What'd you learn, Daniel?' I told him that God wants and deserves so much more than I've surrendered. He wants it all."

My father didn't sugarcoat the call for Christians to get up off their sofas, away from whatever junk they were obsessed with on TV, and look at the bigger world around them. He liked to quote Matthew 5:13–14, about how we are the salt of the earth and the light of the world, about how we shouldn't ask if this is a role for us because God has already given us this role. It's not an *option* for us, but an *expectation* from God.

"As you wait before the Lord, asking God to bring his person of choice for you to minister to and serve with, know that he or she may come from what the religious community would call an 'unclean' place," he wrote. "Think of those whom Jesus loved— the lepers, the tax collectors, the beggars, the prostitutes.

"Jesus went to the place called Sychar in the heart of Samaria, an area considered unclean by most God-fearing people. Great racial prejudice was held against these people by the religious establishment. Yet the Scripture says Jesus 'had to pass' through Samaria on his trip from Judea to Galilee. Although most 'good, religious people' of Jesus' time went many miles out of their way to avoid any contact with the people of Samaria, Jesus' route took him straight to the woman at the well."

Often, my dad would personalize the Kenyan experience for this time and place. "Just for a minute," he said, "close your eyes and imagine something with me. Imagine one million people living on top of each other in one square mile. Imagine one toilet for every four hundred people. Imagine men, women, and children rummaging through the refuse searching for something to eat. Now, imagine they are your children. *Then* would you do something?"

Thirty-Eight

THE HOLY ROLLER

:::::

The call came on my dad's cell just as we were heading into one of Grace's swim meets. It was one of his doctors. A routine scan had shown what nobody wanted to know: The cancer had moved into his lymph nodes. He got the call in the parking lot and just broke down in front of Mom and me.

"We're through," is all he said.

It didn't seem fair. He thought he was that one in a million privileged to be a walking, talking miracle of God. But he attended the swim meet anyway and shouted, "Go! Go! Go!" as if he'd not just heard what he'd just heard.

Afterward, outside, he broke the news to Grace.

"But no matter what," he said, "you're my little girl."

The two hugged, melded by tears. Then he insisted that, instead of joining the rest of us for dinner, she stay with her swim squad for their planned team meal.

"You're the captain," he said, and then he took her hand and prayed for her.

That was my dad. "Hardly ever did he make a decision out of selfishness," Grace later said.

The return of his cancer in February 2012 was a bitter fifty-first birthday present for my father. On his blog, he put on a happy face. "We praise God for the good news about two other tests on my esophagus and liver. Both were cancer-free." But alone, and with us, he was crushed.

If his initial response was defeat, however, his counter-response was quite the opposite when doctors outlined seven weeks of treatment for him in Houston. Proton radiation treatment was going to be used to dissolve one of the cancer spots. Chemo was going to be used to shrink the other so it was operable. He would be going to MD Anderson Cancer Center in Houston, Monday through Thursday for nearly two months.

When he got to the center, Dad all but ignored himself and his treatment. Instead, he embraced the experience as a chance to get to know others, encourage others, pray for others, and witness about God's glory.

"Within his first thirty minutes of being there, people knew there was something different about Mike Fechner," said Mike Buster, who took one of the trips to Houston with Dad and Mom. "He believed strongly that you are the church wherever you go."

If Buster hadn't seen Dad "work his magic" in LA, he would have been more surprised. Even then, Dad's boldness with people left Buster—a pastor himself—shaking his head. "He'd spend hours rolling that IV setup from room to room, talking to people, listening to people, praying with people, giving books to people."

Indeed, the IV pole became his staff, as if he were some Old

Testament prophet wandering the wilderness, room by room. Within days, he had established a moveable church of sorts. He was a true Holy Roller, offering prayers and encouragement, not to mention gift cards, tickets to amusement parks for kids, and copies of a go-to book.

In a world full of bestselling authors whose books had sold millions, the one he loved to pass out was a self-published book by a guy who went to Prestonwood, Jon Lineberger, called *What God Did with a Mess Like Me*. It was about a man who'd made all sorts of mistakes—and had been redeemed by God.

"Everything Mike did was as if it was straight from the book of Acts," said Buster. "The disciples turned the world upside down. Mike Fechner turned the world upside down wherever he went. Or better yet, put it right side up."

In the second week, when my father was ushered to the back of a long line to have blood drawn, he noticed a heaviness in the others waiting. The lone exception was the woman on staff who was organizing the people in the line; she did so with a lilt of joyfulness, care, and concern.

When he finished giving his blood, Dad asked if he could have his picture taken with her and tell her manager what a great job she was doing. "She was thrilled that someone would want a picture with her and couldn't wait to oblige," he wrote.

For most people, that would have been bold enough, right? Not for my dad. "After the picture, I had the joy of praying for this marvelous servant, and she said, 'That prayer touched me. That prayer was better than a preacher's prayer.'"

The same day, Dad and two young pastors he knew—guys

who'd driven from Dallas to encourage him—encountered a woman on a shuttle bus, who, like my dad, was being treated for lung cancer. She was distraught. My father asked if he might pray for her. She welcomed the prayer, which was neither silent nor subtle. When the shuttle arrived at the hospital, the bus driver said, "Thanks for the revival on the bus. We need more of that."

By the third week, nobody knew my dad as Mike Fechner, but as "Pastor Mike." He'd arrive in the chemo ward, and the front desk workers would start spreading the word. "Pastor Mike," they'd say, "is in his office."

He was as transparent as a window, and he neither apologized for nor boasted of his tendency to engage complete strangers in the deeper things of life. He could discern a waitress's spiritual condition before she poured his second cup of tea and do the same for a guy on the treadmill next to him at a health club.

True, he was always late to appointments. "I called it Fechner Standard Time," said Mary Anderwald. "I had a lot of twenty-minute visits with people in his office as we waited for him to arrive."

But the reason he was always late wasn't out of disrespect for the people he was going to meet with. "It was because he'd stopped along the way to engage someone in a conversation about their life or to pray for them," said Mike Buster. "People were his priority." The meeting could wait, he figured; someone who needed a personal revival could not.

"I used to joke with him about it," said Mike. "I said, 'Fech, you'll be late for your own funeral.'"

Thirty-Nine

CHEMO CHURCH

:::::

At MD Anderson, my dad would walk into a room and people would flock to him as if he were the mail-call guy during World War II. The draw wasn't Mike Fechner; the draw was encouragement, prayer, laughter, optimism, and hope.

He was a little like that needy guy, Bob (played by Bill Murray), in the movie *What about Bob?* When Dr. Leo Marvin (Richard Dreyfuss) drops him off at the mental hospital, Bob doesn't sink to others' level of depression. Instead, he brings everybody else up to his level of optimism. Within a half hour, Bob is telling jokes to a group of people—doctors and nurses among them—who roar at his every punch line. My dad did the same, only with a spiritual twist.

That's what my father loved about interacting with people. He was just like everybody else—broken, hurting, needy—but people wanted to be around him because he had a solution to rise above the brokenness, the pain, the hurt: Jesus.

"Pretty soon, there'd be doctors in there too," said Buster. "One of them would say, 'Hey, you need to go see this guy in 305.'"

Soon, my dad's ministry in Houston took on an unofficial name: Chemo Church. And for the first time, my siblings and I were able to come to see him. Before, he didn't want us exposed to the inner workings of the whole medical routine, but in April 2012, Jon, seventeen, and Grace, fifteen, not only started coming to Houston but doing ministry there as well.

When he wasn't getting chemo treatments, you see, my father had been slipping into Houston's inner city to an area called the Third Ward, making connections, seeing how he could be used for God. Among the discoveries: One of the young pastors he met in the area had been mentored by no less than E. K. Bailey himself.

"Nineteen years ago, E. K., who is now in heaven, was driving through this same neighborhood," Dad wrote, "and felt convicted by the Holy Spirit to encourage this pastor to lead a church here in the Third Ward, a church that had grown from one hundred fifty people to almost three thousand."

Dad started laying plans to bring a satellite operation of BridgeBuilders to Houston. Meanwhile, Jon and Grace joined him on Saturday mornings in the city's less desirable neighborhoods, along with ministering to folks at the cancer center.

The keys to this happening were twofold. First, my father had learned to mentally knock down the barrier between "us" and "them" when he'd go to an unfamiliar place. "When I go to the inner city, I begin to see these people as my own," he wrote. "Even though I do not live there, the residents become my family because of our shared faith in the Lord."

Second, he always looked for the best in people, regardless of how wrongly they might have acted, how unapproachable they might be, or whether or not they were Christians. Having lung cancer had hammered home a lesson he'd learned in the previous few decades but hadn't internalized until "the Big C" hit.

"Many judge me wrongly regarding my lung cancer," he wrote. "They *assume* I smoked, although I never did. In the same way, many judge the poor as having done something wrong, which caused them to deserve their current position in life. It is interesting that the Pharisees were the group Jesus went after the most, never the sick or the poor. It is our joyous opportunity to be God's light in the darkest places."

Whenever Dad experienced something new, he used it as a learning opportunity. The lust for possessions, he was reminded, fades in a cancer center. "I have never seen anyone in the chemo ward looking at what color they want to use when they redo their house," he said once in a sermon. "I've never seen anyone in the chemo ward looking at sports, going, 'Wow, my team is winning.' I've never seen anyone in the chemo ward shopping for new clothes. The devil is a deceiver and a liar. He wants to get you caught up in your car, your fitness, how you look, your hair, your nails."

Everywhere my father turned, people were donating money for gift cards and books to help Chemo Church patients in Houston. In Dallas, a woman at a shopping mall gave my sister and her friend one hundred dollars each because they had shown her uncommon respect. When they told the woman they were going to donate it to Chemo Church and explained what it was, the woman matched their two hundred dollars with another two hundred dollars.

Back at Prestonwood, people dedicated an entire night to pray for Dad and this new ministry, specifically that the side effects of cancer treatment would not prevent him from connecting with people. "My doctor called me 'the poster child for proton radiation and chemotherapy,'" he wrote.

He didn't care if people thought he was crazy. My dad embraced "crazy" as if it were a badge of honor. He pictured himself a little like David against Goliath. *Yeah, I can take this guy—with God on my side, I can take this guy.* He definitely had an underdog streak, a "rebel with a cause" streak.

Around this time, he started seriously considering uprooting our family and moving to Bonton. He sensed that was where God wanted the family to be, though I'm not sure the rest of the family was as "all in" as he was. At times, sure, Dad was more zealous than the rest of us about ministry, but he never sacrificed us for others. When we needed him, he was always there.

In my brother Daniel's first semester at Texas, his grades were bad and he was close to failing a class. What's more, after blowing a large amount of graduation money that Dad's friends had given him, his car door had been dented to the tune of seven hundred dollars, and he didn't have any money to fix it.

"I was so focused on trying to be successful by the world's standards, and little seemed to be working out," said Daniel. "So Dad leaves in the middle of the week, drives all the way to Austin, has dinner with me, and drives home that night. And what he did was show me the same grace he'd been shown in his life. He spent most of his time encouraging me."

Forty

DARK NIGHT
OF THE SOUL

:::::

As the spring of 2012 arrived, so did a stamp of validation for the work that BridgeBuilders and others had done in Bonton. A major spread in the *Dallas Morning News* called attention to the makeover the slums had been given in the last few decades. "Bonton is changing as pride spreads from street to street," read the headline on page 2.

The people behind it? "The determination of residents like Clifton Reese and Velma Mitchell," wrote the reporter. "Reese and Mitchell are founding members of the fledgling Bonton Neighborhood Association and unlikely allies in the battle against neglect and indifference that pervade the community. He's a reformed drug dealer, and she's the mother of a son killed by a drive-by shooting. But both share a passion for Bonton."[*]

---

[*] Diane Jennings, "Taking Back Bonton Means Making It Home," *Dallas Morning News*, March 10, 2012, 1–2A, http://www.dallasareahabitat.org/c/document_library/get_file?p_l_id=33636&folderId=48594&name=DLFE-1917.pdf (accessed July 27, 2015).

The newspaper pointed out that crime—violent and otherwise—had plummeted. That new houses were being built. That while the place hadn't become a model of perfection, residents had "taken back" their neighborhood.

My father wasn't mentioned. But here's how he prefaced a mention of the story in a March 2012 blog post: "Every miracle you read in this story is only because of Jesus. When the Lord is present, he changes everything . . . Thank you all for joining in this movement of God called H.I.S. BridgeBuilders!"

It was the same way with the cancer. If he wasn't quick to take credit for things he had helped accomplish, neither was he quick to milk his cancer fight for sympathy. But, oh, what a roller-coaster ride it was turning out to be. When the seven-week treatment in Houston ended, Dad awakened one night to excruciating pain in his spine and neck. "It was," he wrote, "one of the darkest nights of my soul."

A scan showed that the roller coaster was plummeting on a steep downward path: a cancerous tumor was discovered elsewhere. My father now had brain cancer.

At Prestonwood, hundreds of people gathered for a special service in which church elders, based on a Bible verse from the book of James, anointed my father with oil and prayed for his healing. "This is not *a wake*," said Pastor Graham. "This is *an awakening*."

Later, my father referred to author Henri Nouwen's definition of the word *obedient*. It is derived from the Latin word *audire*, which means "listening." "When we awaken and learn to listen to God, we become obedient," he wrote. "As we hear from God, we get his heart. And what is his heart? To restore all of creation to himself."

At the prayer service, Daron Babcock spoke. Daron was the successful businessman—a widower—who had made good on his promise and moved from Plano to Bonton. "I didn't give up anything," he said. "God called me to let go of things that were preventing me from experiencing all the goodness he had waiting for me. When I made these decisions, I *felt* like I was giving up a lot, but it's been the greatest gift in the world to walk alongside Mike and the BridgeBuilders staff in this great work of God."

Daron told of a young man from Bonton so poor that one night he asked to spend the night with Daron and his son; the young man's house had no water or electricity and very little food.

The next morning, the young man went to church with Daron and his son. When the pastor invited people to come forward to ask for prayer or share a praise, the young man did so. Daron certainly understood; his young friend needed prayer for difficult life circumstances. But the young man did not ask for prayer for himself.

"There is a man who is helping in my community, Mike, and his ministry is helping my family," he said. "He has brain cancer, and I want you to pray for him."

A few days before his August 2012 brain surgery, my father was having breakfast with his friend Johnson Ellis. With no verbal preface, Dad pulled a ring off his finger—a ring with a cross on it, not his wedding ring—and slid it across the table to Ellis. He said nothing, and Ellis understood.

"Because Mike and I were so close, I realized he was letting me know that he knew the brain surgery was serious," said Ellis. "He might die. And if not, he wasn't sure how long the recovery was going to take and he wanted me to help watch over the ministry and 'the least of these' he loved so dearly—until God restored his health."

The two blinked back tears.

That night, our family gathered for dinner—known today, amid family black humorists, as "the last supper." Dad gave each of us a marker—a ring, or watch or necklace, just a symbol of his love for us. Deep down, I believe he thought he might die, and he wanted to leave each of us a reminder of how much we meant to him.

On August 9, about one hundred people were in the waiting room on the day my father underwent brain surgery. They came to pray, to support, to show they cared. Later, when the surgeon came out, he had good news: The tumor had come out in one piece.

"We all know that somebody else had something to do with this," his doctor said. My father experienced none of the expected nausea or headaches and was free from pain in his neck. "Please quote me on this," said his doctor. "This is a miracle."

Within forty-eight hours of the surgery, my father was spending more time in the waiting room praying with families whose loved ones were undergoing surgery than in his bed. A week after the surgery, he was working out in a gym.

Not that this would be the end of his battle with cancer.

In November, my father joyously took part in an "I Love Bonton" event, sponsored by the new Bonton Neighborhood

Association and punctuated with a beautiful wedding that brought together Clifton Reese's uncle, Milton Baker, and his bride, Grace. My dad insisted the wedding be held outdoors in Bonton to remind others that people in the community were making lifetime commitments to each other in a place where that had been rare.

Milton had met my father the year before when, after serving a prison sentence for armed robbery, the Bonton man returned to the community he'd grown up in. "I heard there's this white guy leading a Bible study in Bonton, and I said, 'I have to see this,'" said Milton. "Sure enough, he was there. And when I walked through that door, it was like God was telling me this is where I need to be."

Dad took Milton out for lunch. "Milton," he asked, "can I walk this walk with you? I'm willing to walk as far as you want to go." It's the promise he'd made to Rodrick Yarbrough and Clifton Reese and many other disciples—a promise he would keep.

"By that point in my life, I know when people are being sincere and when they're shining you on," said Milton. "I recognized that this guy was for real. He could make you feel like you're the only person in the room. He taught me humility, to be a servant, to have compassion for people. When I was in his presence, I became aware that it wasn't about being white or black or Hispanic or Asian."

My father helped Milton study the Bible, buy a car, and, of course, marry Grace in a first-rate style. A few years earlier, Milton had been in prison; nobody trusted him a bit. Today he's trusted with the keys to the BridgeBuilders Economic Development Center; he's the guy who opens the door every morning before anyone else gets there—the caretaker of a multimillion-dollar building.

"I walk into the dark building and I flips the lights on, and I sees Mike's picture on the wall and I says, 'Hey, man, what's going on? Brother Mike, I needs you to be with me today. Love you, bros.'"

Forty-One

BLISS

:::::

By 2013, BridgeBuilders was humming. Tim Tebow, a Heisman Trophy winner, appeared for a March 2013 fund-raiser, and the organization had popular NFL quarterback Peyton Manning lined up for the following spring. Money was flowing in. Leaders were leading. People were getting help at the street level. "I ♥ Bonton" sweatshirts were becoming a new look in the community.

For my father, life, if tenuous, was good. In October 2013, my folks celebrated their thirtieth wedding anniversary by renewing their wedding vows. With friends Johnson and Beth Ellis, they flew to Florida to stay at a posh seaside resort. Thanks to the generosity of friends, the entire trip was paid for, and my father was in a state of bliss.

"Right now, in the last season of my life," he wrote, "I'm in a season of unexplainable joy. Here I am at a resort I can't afford, with friends of deep character I shouldn't by all rights have, with a wife who stuck with me through heaven and hell. I look back at the life I once pursued, at the things I once grasped for, and know that I was a greedy, arrogant, manipulative person. I don't deserve this. The abundance of this good life in this season God has given me today is so much more than I could have built for myself."

Johnson was the one leading the renewing-the-vows service. His wife, Beth, was the only other witness. Johnson sang "Turn Your Eyes Upon Jesus." Pointing to the ocean, Johnson encouraged the two of them to cast into the sea whatever they needed to discard. For my father, the stuff that needed casting was, in his words, "all our past failures. (Mine are huge.) All our harsh words. (There have been plenty.) All the impatience. All the shortcomings. All fears of abandonment. All fears about health issues. (Something we struggle with daily, even today.)"

They repeated their vows. And kissed.

Bliss, indeed. That's what my folks were experiencing after all their triumphs and trials. Grace, seventeen, was off visiting colleges. Jonathan, who had just turned nineteen, had postponed his first year of college to work in BridgeBuilders' inner-city ministry in Buffalo. Daniel, twenty-two, had passed up a commercial banking offer from a well-reputed bank and was serving the Lord in the Middle East. And Caitlin and I were starting our married life—she serving as a counselor at a Christian school, me running a fledgling awning business that employed Bonton men. Both of us were involved in mentoring ministries, and we adopted an inner-city football team whose kids didn't have much support.

It was an introspective time for Dad, a time to look back and consider who he had been and who he had become. He didn't worry much about where he was going. He knew.

As he sat there in Florida, he marveled at how some people

who, if they saw him and Mom in this lavish resort, might think him to be the owner of some Fortune 500 company. "I'm a nobody," he wrote. "So even I can't understand why the state's attorney general, a week before our trip, hung on my every word. I have no position of significance in this country and yet I've spoken at the White House and one of the presidents knows me by name. Why is it that the organization that I helped start is staffed with some of the nation's sharpest executives—men and women who used to command seven-figure salaries and yet have given up their businesses to come work with me?

"This is my story, the great reversal. My life is not about living out a prosperity gospel; it's about being poor in spirit. It's about knowing that God longs to bless us with the abundant, good life—but it may not be the good life we've always imagined. We've been taught that we need to strive and claw and climb and step over people and achieve and own everything ourselves. I don't strive anymore. Yet I'm living the best life I could possibly live.

"I once drove BMWs and a Mercedes; now I drive an Acura. Or I drive an old pickup truck that the ministry has. I don't give a rip. If it goes, it goes. Praise God."

Mom had the same priorities. In fact, when BridgeBuilders was experiencing some financial challenges, she voluntarily sold her own car to help keep the ministry afloat.

As the plane taking them home from Florida approached Dallas/Fort Worth International Airport, my father looked down to see the Bonton community he loved and the Plano community where he lived. "North Dallas. South Dallas. Two cities. Same name. Go to a school in North Dallas, and you'll see marching bands and matching uniforms and high school stadiums. Go to a school in South Dallas, and you'll see rusted bleachers and used syringes and condoms on the ground. That's our people, Laura's and mine. The ones in South Dallas."

He had reconciled within himself that he and Mom should soon move to Bonton. "His heart was in the inner city," said Jarrett Stephens, the Prestonwood teaching pastor. "He ultimately wanted to move down there. Wanted to immerse himself in the place."

Forty-Two

THE FINAL SEASON

:::::

As if having teased my father into a sense of triumph, the cancer came back. Between October 2012 and July 2013, my father had three small surgeries, and by the fall of 2013, he was like a boxer who'd been knocked down and was struggling to get up. Literally.

He switched doctors and hospitals a couple of times. Some physicians offered Hail Mary attempts to prolong his life, but these so-called solutions—one was whole-brain radiation— seemed worse than the disease itself. For the first time, Dad shook his head sideways. No more surgeries. No more treatments.

It was time to let go. Time to say, "Enough."

Mike Buster wouldn't stand for that. Same with some other folks. They insisted Dad keep allowing more of these temporary "fixes." He couldn't give up. He just couldn't. But my father said he wasn't giving up; he was trusting God. "I don't want to live from hospital visit to hospital visit," he said. "God is going to either heal me or take me."

On October 31, 2013, he sent an e-mail to extended family members: "Today we canceled our doctor appointments and next scans. There is a sweet peace in my heart as we rest completely in the arms of our loving Jesus."

Later, in an interview, he found it interesting that 90 percent of his "more affluent friends, the ones with resources," disagreed with his decision to *not* seek further treatment. "[But] amazingly, all of my Kenyan friends are completely behind it. They say, 'Now you have faith.'

"People protect what they know, a doctrine or a status quo or a mind-set or a system or a structure, instead of trusting in a God who works in mysterious and wondrous ways," he wrote.

If Dad survived cancer, God would get the glory. And he loved the idea that he could be used by God for something so grand.

But when he realized his time was short, he drew parallels between his life and that of E. K. Bailey, of whom he once said, "E. K.'s time was appointed. He had fulfilled his role in bringing glory to God. The seed has a season. One plants, one waters, one reaps." E. K. had planted. Someone else, perhaps Bryan Carter, would be the one who now reaps.

After Christmas came and went, we were afraid to leave Dad alone because he hadn't been sleeping well and was getting disoriented. Grace and Mom went to Stillwater, Oklahoma, to check out Oklahoma State as a university for my sister. While they were gone, Dad stayed at our house. He didn't sleep that night, and in the morning, when getting dressed, Dad fell. Caitlin was the one who found him and had to call an ambulance.

He was never the same after that.

On January 22, 2014, in an interview with a family doctor,

he described in detail his cough, blurred vision, and difficulty sleeping. "I want to get all these symptoms recorded because whenever the healing comes, others can know how much the Lord has done." Dad remained full of joy and optimism, regardless of the fate that likely awaited him. But he wondered if what was causing these symptoms was bronchitis, not cancer.

The interview was sprinkled with moments of his breaking into tears. "It's so amazing to see your wife with you, your children, joining with you in the ministry. I have no regrets. There's no going back. I wouldn't trade a single day of what God's given to me." He praised God for giving him fifty-five months, not the maximum eighteen he'd originally been told by a doctor. "I just want everybody to know that God is the real deal," he said. "He's who he says he is."

Then, somewhat surprisingly, he switched topics, to Bonton. "When I get through this, I'm moving to Bonton. It's taken me too long to get there . . . Our house is still too nice for us to live in for what I do. Friday I'm going to meet with a builder about building us a house down there and getting rid of this trash."

Mom and Dad had talked about it for a while, but Mom didn't think it was fair to not let Grace finish her senior year at Prestonwood Academy. It was January. She would graduate in May. Somewhere, Jonathan's words must have echoed in my father's mind: *Dad, you got to make it through Grace's senior year. She needs you.*

Meanwhile, I decided we needed to bring Daniel back from overseas and Jon, who was interning in Buffalo, back from New

York for Dad's birthday on February 3. I wanted all of us to be with him during what we thought could be Dad's final season.

On the way home from the airport with my brothers, I updated them. "Dad's not the same," I said. "Throughout his fight for the last few years, he's still been the same guy he's always been. But in the last few weeks, he's really gone downhill. Hardly any energy. Hardly sleeping. Doesn't talk much. Just so you know."

When we got home, I went in by myself and told Dad we had a surprise birthday present for him. "Close your eyes," I said.

He was sitting in his favorite chair. I waved in Jonathan and Daniel. "OK, open your eyes."

He looked up, and his eyes moistened and he just cried. He didn't say a word. Later, he hugged Daniel and Jonathan and Grace. He stretched out his hand to me and placed it against my face and wept.

We took Dad to the doctor a few days later—the whole family plus Mike Buster and Johnson Ellis. The doctor, after seeing the scans, said it wasn't bronchitis that was causing the coughing and lack of sleep; it was cancer. The doctor's words were vindicating for Dad because he had been second-guessing himself for having given up on further treatments a few months back. The doctor said he would have done the same thing had it been him; the treatment wouldn't have been pretty.

The doctor said he could give Dad some drugs, mostly steroids, that would help ease the pain down the stretch. My father nodded yes amid sobs.

"How long does he have?" someone asked.

"Weeks, not months," the doctor said. "I'm sorry."

We all went to lunch at a taco place, and it was like we were at the Cheesecake Factory all over again, only this time we were all a little more seasoned, a little more prepared. We cried together on the way to the restaurant, at the restaurant, and on the way home from the restaurant.

By now, wet eyes were becoming standard fare for us all. When Grace swam at the state swim meet in San Antonio, the whole family came to cheer her on. Tired, Dad found it difficult to sit in the bleachers. But when Grace's relay event started, there he was.

"I looked up in the stands, and he was sitting there with the biggest smile on his face," said Grace. "I knew I had to swim my heart out."

She did. Though Prestonwood Christian Academy's 400-freestyle team had fallen behind, Grace, swimming the anchor leg, posted a lifetime-best time to rally the girls to a comeback win.

Later, she and Dad hugged. They cried. Seeing them, I cried. We all cried.

We all knew such moments had become "limited time only" offers.

Forty-Three

TAKING LEAVE

:::::

As word spread that my father's time was fading fast, people wanted
to say good-bye. People he had discipled. Businessmen. Ministers
from around the country. Extended family. Friends. Folks from
Bonton. All coming by to say good-bye. And thank you.

Clifton Reese, the drug dealer turned Bible study mentor,
was having trouble accepting the reality that his adopted father
could die. "I always trusted him completely," he said. "If I'd
been on the far side of the world and I needed him, I knew he
would be there for me. I truly thought he was Superman."

Clifton called my father "Dad" or "Pa" and my mother
"Mama." In March, he showed up one afternoon with his ten-
year-old son Arnaz. "We were sitting back by the pool. Dad
puts his arm around Arnaz and says, 'I'm your granddaddy,' and
smiles. Our kids was his kids. And it works both ways. I know
my last name's Reese, but I'm a Fechner." I always considered
that an honor—to have someone think so highly of our family
that he'd attach himself to us like that.

In the weeks to come, a dozen visitors became two dozen.

Two dozen became four. I'm sure that, ultimately, more than a hundred came.

"This was the only point in his life he had trouble talking, and it physically wore him out to meet with them, but he wanted to keep challenging them," said my brother Daniel. "He knew they would experience abundant life if they continued to surrender more, and he wasn't shy in telling them that."

Before the brain surgery, Dad had given markers to all of us in the family—reminders that if he didn't make it through, he loved us. Now, as the end neared, he had one more gift to give—to the quiet hero of his story. Mom had been out running errands, and when she returned home, nearly a dozen of her and Dad's friends were in the living room with a surprise they'd all chipped in on.

With tears streaming down Dad's face, he began to read her a letter:

Dear Laura,

Because of your servant heart and the way you have sacrificially given, I wanted to do something for you. There are not many women who would be willing to sell their car to support our family and our ministry. You have shown over the years that your heart is of the kingdom of God and not of this world. Because you would never ask for yourself, it was my joy to ask for you, from people who love you . . .

It was outside waiting for her—a brand-new Ford Explorer, a gift from people who loved my mom dearly, none more than my father.

"You are the best ministry partner I could have," my dad continued amid sniffles, "and I am humbled by your sacrificial life. We all love you and want you to know how much you mean to us."

Dad wanted to show his appreciation for her supporting him through the selling of their "American Dream" business; through the highs and lows of giving away all their money; through starting a ministry for the poor; and through walking beside him during almost five years of cancer treatment.

It was only later that I began noticing the common theme in people's good-bye stories when they came to see him. Almost to a person, here's what they said: *I came to say good-bye and to encourage him, and he wound up saying good-bye to me and encouraging me to continue to fight the fight.*

"He's lying on his back in a lounge chair, and he grabs my hand and says, 'Would you like to pray?'" said Matthew McIntyre, a close friend of my father's. "And then he spends fifteen minutes blessing *me*."

A few of Prestonwood's young pastors stopped by. My dad good-naturedly rebuked them for not praying enough, as if E. K. Bailey were laughing heartily from heaven and saying, "So you've turned into that prayer curmudgeon I was, Mike. I love it! See you soon, brother!"

Two weeks before he died, Dad took another nosedive. He continued meeting people at the house, but only those closest to him. My father wept at nearly every such meeting. Three days before he died, he heard from a friend whose son wanted my father to baptize him. My dad didn't hesitate, sending for a basin and baptizing the guy's son at our house.

On Wednesday, April 9, 2014, while I was at work, Mom called. The hospice nurse had told her Dad had only a few days left. Mom sobbed on the phone. I told her I loved her and that I would take the next couple of days off to be at the house. I stopped by Mom and Dad's house late that afternoon, just to check in for the day before spending the next couple of days at the house with Dad.

Returning home that night, I began to process what the next few days might entail. Then the phone rang. It was Jonathan. He was crying. "Dad just died," he said.

"I'm coming," I said. "I love you."

Caitlin and I headed to the house. On the way, I called Mike Buster. He was in disbelief. He said he'd make calls and be there shortly.

When I got to the house, Mom, Grace, Daniel, and Jon were huddled together on the sofa, sobbing hard. I joined them.

"I thought we had a few more days," Mom kept saying.

It hurt to see her hurt. But I'd heard that, before I arrived, Dad had looked up and seen my mother and, with all the strength he could muster, broke into a grin.

"You are so beautiful," he said.

Now he was gone. We might not have gotten that "final words" moment, but we had told him we loved him every day. There was nothing left to say.

Dad died in his bedroom in his sleep. The breathing slowed and slowed and, finally, was no more. Everybody was there but me.

People started arriving. Hugs. Tears. Prayers. Mumbled words. I went into the bedroom, and there he was—my hero. I touched his hands, kissed his forehead, and rubbed his face one more time. Then a few others came in to say good-bye. As they filed out, it was just the family left in the room with Dad, the once-cocky millionaire who had given it all to the poor.

One by one, we kissed him, told him we loved him, and walked out. Mom was last. She said good-bye to her husband, the man who dared to change. Who, by living out the principles he preached, taught us to do the same. And who on the funeral home's information sheet had not only checked "Flowers Accepted" but scrawled a short message that echoed a last laugh.

"And cheesecake."

Forty-Four

GOOD-BYE

:::::

As Mike Buster had predicted years before, my father was, indeed, late for his own funeral. His friends all agreed that his closed casket needed to be wheeled into Prestonwood Baptist Church a good ten minutes after the service had begun, just to honor him and "Fechner Standard Time."

The ninety-minute service drew an estimated 2,500 people. "We have had large funerals at our church—Dallas Cowboys players, famed businessmen, and celebrities among them—but Mike's was the largest in the history of the church," said Buster. "He was not a celebrity, but he influenced more people than anyone I've ever known."

Prestonwood people. Nurses and patients from MD Anderson in Houston. Folks from Bonton, though the community would pay tribute to my dad in a separate service as well. Titans of Dallas business. Ex-cons such as Hector, who wept throughout the service.

My father touched so many people because when he looked at millionaires, he didn't see their money, but their hearts. And when he looked at guys such as Hector, he didn't see their tattoos, but their potential.

One of his former interns, Jarrett Stephens, told the funeral attendees how Dad "was drawn like a magnet to the poor, the widow, the orphan. He loved the poor because he found them to be rich in faith."

Dad's older brother Ruben talked of my father's thirst for variety—that he truly found it to be the spice of life. "He did not limit himself to the people of one denomination, one race, one ethnicity. He did not limit his time and place to this complex, to the city of Dallas, to Texas, to even the United States. God removed those limits as [Mike] embraced the beautiful variety of life."

Von Minor, copastor with my father of Restoration Community Church, told the audience that if my dad were still here, he would implore us to go out to serve the poor and proclaim Jesus.

Jack Graham said the truest test of my father's faith was when the cancer hit, and instead of being blown off course, my father actually deepened his walk with God and his outreach to others.

Then there was me. Nobody encouraged me, the former mumbler, to get up in front of 2,500 people at the most heartbroken point in my life. But I did it. For *him*—a man worthy of honor. For the guy who loved me enough to encourage me, to teach me, to gently pull me out of my hermit shell of insecurity and show me I could speak in front of a crowd. Speaking at his funeral was my way of thanking my dad for making me the man I am.

Like nearly all the other speakers, I didn't get through without an emotional lurch or two—and I'm sure Dad would have approved, given that he could weep over some "home for Christmas" TV commercial. I talked about how he would embarrass the family in public places with great regularity. For instance, he yelled, "Shamu, Shamu, we're here!" when we first got to SeaWorld in San Antonio. I mentioned that he would pick me up from school, ostensibly for "lunch," but then take me to Bonton to do ministry together. I told them that only four days before he died, we placed a video camera in front of him and asked what one thing he wanted to leave us with.

He sat in front of that camera for forty-five minutes. Tired. Listless. On the verge of death. Finally he said, "We . . . need . . . to . . . have . . . an . . . awakening."

I told the audience how I played on a young marrieds softball team—our name was just that, "Awakening"—and how Dad would be the only parent to show up. "I think he came just so he could shout it over and over, as loud as he could: 'Awakening! Awakening! Awakening!'"

He knew all about awakenings. And if anyone doubted they could happen, he'd tell about a selfish, "me first, have it all" fellow who fit so perfectly into upscale Plano, Texas, back in the 1980s.

He wasn't that man anymore.

And he wasn't the feeble guy sitting in front of a video camera.

He was my father. And he took me, our family, and all who knew him on an incredible, twenty-five-year mission trip unlike any other I can imagine.

:::::

The burial was at Hillcrest Sparkman Cemetery in Dallas. A few songs were sung. At Dad's request, the final one was "In Times Like These," sung by Velma Mitchell.

It was the song she had been singing that night in Bonton twenty-five years earlier when the scales had fallen off my father's eyes and he saw himself for who he really was—a pretender.

The song sung both times by a woman who taught him so much about prayer and fasting, who opened up a new world to him among Bonton's poor, who helped change his life.

The song that brings to mind Velma's mother, who told her children that, like a single stick, alone, we can easily be broken. But together, with those around us, with God in us, with the Holy Spirit working through us, we cannot be broken, even by death itself.

Forty-Five

THE LEGACY

:::::

Two *days after* my father died, the doorbell rang at our house. There stood Milton Baker, the man from Bonton who'd spent more than two decades in jail for armed robbery, the man my father had helped start over. He broke into tears and hugged my mother like he never wanted to let go.

The power of my father's life isn't found in anything he accomplished, but in changed lives. "Mike's fingerprints are still everywhere I look," said his friend Kevin O'Neal.

In people such as Milton, who once was lost but now was found. In the way Sharon Emmert went from serving drinks to comfortable people on a jetliner to serving the poor in South Dallas. In so many others, touched by him directly or touched by those he had touched.

Once, at Prestonwood, a young woman saw Velma Mitchell and threw herself into the woman's arms, sobbing with joy and thanking her for how she had inspired her. She had been among the young people on the Colorado trip the time Velma had posed as a homeless woman and then spoke to the kids as herself, Velma Mitchell. The young woman told Velma that she had been convicted about her resistance to the "homeless woman" who had accompanied the youth group to Colorado. The young woman had changed her outlook on people because of that incident. This was a learning opportunity that my father had cooked up—not to be controversial, but to lovingly shake up kids and help them understand God's love for everyone.

"I had no idea I'd made that kind of difference in her," said Velma.

My dad called it "the power of one." He wrote that "the power of a relationship with Jesus Christ" can change others in amazing ways.

"Everybody he touched was more kingdom-minded than before they met him," said Mary Anderwald.

Mary knew the "Old Mike," the one bent on getting rich, then richer. On Mom and Dad's twentieth wedding anniversary, guests were asked how to best describe my dad. "*Changed*," Mary said. Dad was living proof that people can change. And when people change, they have the power to inspire others to change.

"He had the authentic heart of a lion," said Matthew McIntyre.

Nearly a year after Dad's death, Jarrett Stephens still couldn't bear to erase Dad's voice mails from his cell phone. Nor could Milton enter the BridgeBuilders building each morning without looking at my father's photo on the wall and acknowledging him.

He helped build BridgeBuilders, yes, but my father's legacy isn't so much about an organization as about the throngs of people he discipled as he helped establish it.

"We're all united in how Mike touched us," said Johnson

Ellis. "We saw something authentic in him. He had his flaws, he had his weaknesses, but his authenticity, to me, was his family. This is a family that, through the high highs and the low lows, greatly honors Christ."

"I used to say if I had just an ounce of what that man had, an ounce of his faith, I'd be doing good," said Clifton Reese.

As for me, I have walked with my father through the halls of the White House, the Valley of Galati in Romania, and the streets of Bonton. My father was a great man, not because he was brilliant or a strategic mastermind, but because he took the simple command of Christ—to love the Lord and to love others—to heart.

Since his passing, there's hardly a day goes by that someone who knew my dad won't tell me, "I miss your dad every single day." The void of his love left a hole in many, including me, but Dad taught us whom to rely on to fill every need—our heavenly Father.

Loving the unlovable is not popular. It's not taught in most seminaries. It's not encouraged by many religious leaders, most of whom would rather have a theological debate or preach a sermon. But my dad's story is a story of love. God loved my dad and saved him from himself. In turn, my dad grew in love for God and began loving those whom God loved.

One of the most important lessons Dad taught me is that if you love others and serve them, they will see the hope of Christ in you. They will want the abundant life you hold. Self-centered faith is an unattractive, unfulfilling faith. But a loving, gracious, serving-others faith leads to fulfillment and salvation for those around you.

While battling cancer, my father once wrote, "I may not be alive to see this story published." Unfortunately, he was right. But his story, your story, my story—they all will live on, long after we're gone, like ripples on the water.

The only question is, "What will our stories be?"

EPILOGUE

::::

- BridgeBuilders has grown into a leading ministry in the quest to end poverty and promote flourishing communities. What started as a Bible study in an old housing development has launched dozens of inner-city missions across America and the globe to build God's kingdom. After Dad died in 2014, Michael Craven ultimately succeeded him as president of BridgeBuilders.

- Velma Mitchell is retired from H.I.S. BridgeBuilders, the ministry she cofounded and helped build. She lives in the Bonton community she helped to rebuild and continues working with the community's nonprofits to bring restoration to her community.

- Clifton Reese works for Nature Nate's Honey Company and leads the Bonton Honey division of the company. Clifton and his family continue to live in, and restore, Bonton. He is still my brother. He is as close to me as Daniel and Jonathan and Grace. They know it. I know it. Clifton is right. He's a Fechner.

- Rodrick Yarbrough recently finished barber school at the top of his class and is working toward his goal of opening his own barber shop in Bonton. He continues to lead men in the community toward the higher calling of Christ.

- Hector Garcia lives in Bonton and serves at Restoration Community Church, where he is a charter member.

- Sheila Bailey leads Sheila B. Ministries, where she mentors and advocates for ministers' wives. She is a prolific author, speaker, and teacher of God's Word.

- Mary Anderwald, Dad's longtime assistant at Prestonwood and BridgeBuilders, continues to serve at BridgeBuilders. Most importantly, she is a strong prayer warrior for God's kingdom.

- Laura Fechner, my mother, still works with BridgeBuilders and carries on the work she and my dad started. My mom was, and continues to be, a strong anchor for our family. Her faith in times of need and sorrow is truly remarkable.

- My brother Daniel works in the banking industry and volunteers frequently with the BridgeBuilders youth sports program. Daniel is a man of strong conviction and integrity and continues to pursue the kingdom through his work in finance.

- My other brother, Jon, is a student at Dallas Baptist University. Beyond being a self-described "ladies' man," he has the prestigious honor of working for the vice president of the university. Jon is a loving and joyful man of God who will never leave you without a smile.

- My sister, Grace, is a student at Oklahoma State University, where she is a Chi Omega. She has an incredible heart for people, a trait she easily picked up from—where else?—our dad. Dad didn't make her high school graduation, as Jon had so fervently hoped, but she knows—we all know—he's still with us in spirit.

- My wife, Caitlin, is a school counselor in the Dallas area and an incredible servant of the Lord. She is a rock when I am shaky and a shoulder to lean on. Most importantly, she is who God has blessed me to love.

- Me? I am a law student at Southern Methodist University and continue teaching and sharing the Word of God at both Prestonwood and in Bonton. More importantly, I am, and will always be, my father's son.

ACKNOWLEDGMENTS

::::

I am humbled by the opportunity to share Dad's story, and it wouldn't have been possible without the help of so many people.

Mary Anderwald, my dad's longtime assistant, helped coordinate and collect an overwhelming amount of data, beyond adding her own keen insight about my father because she knew him so well.

Matt McIntyre, Jarrett Stephens, Rodrick Yarbrough, Mike Buster, Johnson Ellis, Chris Tedford, Kevin O'Neal, Josh Rolf, Clifton Reese, Sheila Bailey, and Velma Mitchell all provided countless hours of interview material. Thank you!

My mom, Laura; my brothers Daniel and Jonathan; and my sister, Grace, have shared memories and helped edit various parts of the copy. I wouldn't have taken on this project without their full support and encouragement. I am humbled they have given me the opportunity to tell Dad's story, *our* story.

Thank you to my wife, Caitlin. While my writing this book took many early mornings, weekends, and nights, she was always by my side to offer advice and provide memories that my small mind had forgotten.

Finally, I must mention Bob Welch, my friend and fellow

writer, who sifted through volumes of journals to format Dad's crazy life in a somewhat linear manner. Trying to accomplish this without Bob's help would have been an exercise in futility. Thank you, Bob, for all your hard work and, Sally, for encouraging him along the way.

Appendix

QUOTES FROM MY FATHER

:::::

- "How tragic it is to spend our lives focusing on such small subjects as ourselves. I continue to be convicted by the amount of need globally and the excess locally."

- "So often, we judge before listening."

- "Great trial actually brings great opportunity."

- "I found that the view isn't pretty while looking up from the lowest economic stratum of American society."

- "Our gospel is not a comfortable gospel, but a gospel of taking up a cross, denying self, and following Jesus."

- "God's way, not yours, is always best."

- "I had faith in Jesus, but my faith was still transactional, not transformational. I liked Jesus because of what he could do for *me*."

- "You've got to die before you truly live."

- "Why should we care about the loss of children being shot and children becoming drug addicts because they are fatherless? Is it our responsibility to be father and mother to the parentless? The undeniable answer God was speaking into my heart was *yes*."

- "There is tremendous fellowship in suffering, and only in suffering do you experience this fellowship."

- "In all this hopelessness, Jesus is more than enough. The faith of so many of the Kenyans in these horrific conditions is humbling. I must confess that I am undone by their godliness and contentment."

- "You've got to love others in order to truly live."

- "The least in the world's eyes are actually the greatest in God's eyes."

- "Many judge the poor as having done something wrong, which caused them to deserve their current position in life. It is interesting that the Pharisees were the group that Jesus went after the most, never the sick or the poor."

- "People protect what they know—a doctrine or a status quo or a mind-set or a system or a structure—instead of trusting in a God who works in mysterious and wondrous ways."

- "E. K.'s time was appointed. He had fulfilled his role in bringing glory to God. The seed has a season. One plants, one waters, one reaps."

- "This is my story, the great reversal. My life is not about living out a prosperity gospel; it's about being poor in spirit. It's about knowing that God longs to bless us with the abundant, good life, but it may not be the good life we've always imagined. We've been taught that we need to strive and claw and climb and step over people and achieve and own everything ourselves. I don't strive anymore. Yet I'm living the best life I could possibly live."

- "Every breath is a gift, every inhalation a promise."

- "We need an awakening."

STUDY OR BOOK CLUB QUESTIONS

Designed for Six Sessions

::::

Chapters 1–6

1. Looking back, Mike described the twentysomething version of himself as "All showroom. No warehouse." What do you think he meant by that? Which of the two does our culture seem to favor, and why?

2. In the 1940s, Mike's mother, as a teenager, was scolded by her father for buying a Coke for the family's African-American maid. When she argued that it was wrong for the woman to be refused service at a drugstore, he said, "It may not be right, but it is the way things are." Does Scripture support him?

3. What pieces did Dr. Jack Graham and Mike Buster supply for the Mike Fechner puzzle?

4. What did Mike admire about Velma Mitchell that triggered an about-face in his life?

Chapters 7–13

1. Velma Mitchell knew she would experience some scorn for joining Prestonwood Baptist Church in upscale Plano. Why, then, did she do so? When was the last time you purposely stepped into an uncomfortable situation? What were the results?

2. Mike experienced the deaths of three people that hit him hard. Did one do more than the others to help him make a life change? If so, which one and why?

3. When Velma arrived to speak at the home of an upscale North Dallas couple, some of the guests mistook her for a maid. What can you learn from the faulty assumptions that were made about Velma?

4. Getting to know Velma and the Bonton community changed Mike's perspective on the divide between haves and have-nots. What are some of the things he learned? Why did it take a shift in his life to learn them?

Chapters 14–20

1. The author uses the illustration of a daredevil who is prepared to ride a bicycle on a tightrope across Niagara Falls. What's the catch? And what's the lesson for followers of Jesus?

2. Mike did some research on the giving habits of the well-off people living in his Plano zip code versus the generosity of people living in Bonton. What did he find? What does it suggest about the people in each zip code area?

3. At one point, Mike headed up a campaign to raise money to build a huge church in an upscale area while at the same time helping the poor in Bonton. Did that discrepancy bother you? Why or why not?

4. E. K. Bailey didn't appreciate people who would say, sometimes with a touch of self-righteousness, "I don't see color." Why did that bother him? Do you agree?

5. What were the two questions E. K. Bailey said Mike should always ask when entering a new relationship? How do you react to these questions?

Chapters 21–32

1. Velma Mitchell and Sharon Emmert were, in the words of Mike Fechner Sr., "like oil and water." And yet he sent them to a conference together, and they came back friends. What are the lessons here?

2. As Rodrick's buddies looked on, what happened to suggest that Mike truly cared about Rodrick and was not just blowing smoke when he said he'd be there for him? Why is it so important to walk the talk?

3. After Rodrick gave his shoes and Dallas Cowboys hat to a down-and-outer in London, Mike said, "The man with the least had given the most." Where is that concept found in the Bible? Can you think of similar biblical examples of such actions?

4. One of the U.S. missionaries in Romania said of the gypsies, "We don't have time to meet all the needs. We're

just preaching the gospel." How did Mike react to that? Was his reaction justified?

Chapters 33–40

1. When Mike learned he had terminal cancer, he wrestled with God about the prognosis. Discuss a time when you felt you were the victim of unfair circumstances. Even if your trial was not as intense as a cancer diagnosis, can you relate to Mike's feelings about perceived injustice? What did you learn from the situation you faced?

2. In terms of readership, Mike's dead-in-the-water blog skyrocketed after people learned he had cancer. What does this say about why God might allow pain and suffering in our lives?

3. Mike Buster tells of Mike Fechner having referred to Jesus' interactions with Zaccheus in terms of outreach. What point did he make?

4. What did Mike Buster mean when he said, about Mike, "He believed strongly that you are the church wherever you go"?

Chapters 41–45

1. When Mike and Laura Fechner were flying home after renewing their marriage vows in Florida, Mike looked down and saw South Dallas and North Dallas. Where was his heart, and why? Had he beaten the cancer, do you believe he would have moved to Bonton?

2. As he neared death, Mike Fechner drew a parallel between himself and E. K. Bailey in terms of life's seasons—sowing and reaping. What was his point?

3. After Clifton came to say good-bye to Mike, the man he had unofficially adopted as his father, he said, "I know my name's Reese, but I'm a Fechner." How might we relate that to our adoption by our heavenly Father?

4. The author ends the book by saying our individual stories "will go on, long after we're gone. The only question is, 'What will our stories be?'" Have you considered what your story will be? If it seems like an unattainable story now, what changes might be necessary to make it a reality?

H.I.S. BRIDGEBUILDERS
hope in salvation

H.I.S. BridgeBuilders is a leading pioneer in urban missions, uniting Christians to alleviate poverty by working to restore people to God, themselves, others, and creation, thereby breaking the cycle of generational poverty. To learn more, visit www.hisbridgebuilders.org.

S. Michael Craven, President

2075 W. Commerce Street
Dallas, Texas 75208
469.621.5960 (Asst.)
hisbridgebuilders.org

"Blessed is the one who considers the poor" (Psalm 41)!

::::